The Anglo~ Irish Novel

The Anglo~ Irish Novel

VOLUME ONE
The Nineteenth Century

John Cronin

APPLETREE PRESS
BELFAST

First published in Northern Ireland by
The Appletree Press Ltd
7 James Street South
Belfast BT2 8DL
1980

ISBN 0 904651 339

The publisher acknowledges the financial
assistance of the Arts Council of Northern
Ireland in the publication of this volume.

Contents

Introduction

My main aim has been to explore in some detail a number of important Irish novels of the nineteenth century, in the belief that these works deserve such analysis in their own right and for the light they throw on their period. Broadly speaking, the works I have chosen could be said to fall roughly into the two categories which Yeats identified when he published his *Irish Representative Tales* in 1891. He there recognised what he called 'two different accents, the accent of the gentry and the less polished accent of the peasantry and those close to them'. Just as well, perhaps, that he hedged a bit in his definition of that second group: Maria Edgeworth and William Carleton fit obviously enough the two extremes Yeats has defined but a middle-class figure like Gerald Griffin belongs a little uneasily somewhere in between and, as we shall see, the fact that he inhabited a sort of social 'no-man's-land' had its effects on even his most successful work. I have tried to place the chapters on individual novels in some sort of constructive context by offering in each case a brief account of the writer's career and, in addition, a short Selected Bibliography of each writer, which is intended to suggest some further reading to anyone interested enough to wish to read on. For reasons of space, these sections have been kept fairly brief but, as is generally the case, some of the works listed in the Selected Bibliographies contain extensive further information for anyone who wishes to read more widely in the field.

The time-span of the works considered, ranging as it does from *Castle Rackrent* in 1800 to *The Real Charlotte* in 1894, covers the century itself and I would hope that it may prove a stimulus to the raising of important questions about a wide range of issues in connection with the fiction itself and its developing relation to its period. Among such issues, one might point particularly to the complex matter of the writer's concept of his audience at any give time. There is not in existence, as far as I know, any comprehensive study of the nature of the audience for Irish fiction in the nineteenth century, no work comparable in its kind to Q. D. Leavis's *Fiction and the Reading Public*. It may be, of course, that the ground has not yet been sufficiently prepared for such a study by adequate accounts of some of the more important individual figures. It is matter for surprise, for example, that no fully comprehensive biographical and critical study of William Carleton, generally accounted the major figure among the native Irish writers of the first half of the century, has yet appeared. A full investigation of the nature and extent of the audience for Irish fiction in the nineteenth century would necessarily involve coverage of both the English and the American markets for such work, and some slight indication of the difficulties awaiting the researcher in this field were suggested by David H. Greene, of New York University, in a brief but stimulating article which he published in the *Irish Times* of 15 March, 1976. Greene identifies there a large American public for the works of Maria Edgeworth, Charles Lever and Samuel Lover, all, he says, 'published by prestigious American firms'. He contrasts the publishers' treatment of these three writers with their attitude to other Irish novelists:

> It is a lesson in the development of literary reputations to compare these three Irish novelists with some of their countrymen. William Carleton, John and Michael Banim and Gerald Griffin were, of course, Catholics and thus identified with the Irish masses. American publishers evidently expected that these novelists would appeal to Americans of the same nationality and class, which meant Irish immigrants with unsophisticated literary tastes who would not in any event be book buyers. And so such novelists were published by smaller, "Catholic" publishers like P. F. Collier, D. & J. Sadleir and P. J. Kennedy whose offices were in the religious goods district near St Peter's Church in lower Manhattan. All one has to do is compare the splendid forty-volume edition of Lever with the three-volume editon of Carleton's novels and tales which was crudely illustrated and printed in double columns on newsprint, published by Collier in 1882, to learn something about the sociology of literary taste and the publishing industry in nineteenth century America.

Greene goes on to describe a particular edition of Gerald Griffin's novel, *The Collegians,* which further suggests the difficulties inherent in any attempt to estimate either literary reputation or the motivation of publishers:

> One edition of "The Collegians", for example, carried an allegorical frontispiece illustration from an unidentified medieval manuscript representing "the discords existing between the different classes of society". The introduction was written by James, Cardinal Gibbons, and informed the reader that Griffin's novel emphasised "the peace and happiness and content resulting from wisely contracted Christian marriage and conjugal fidelity, and likewise the dreadful evils that ill-assorted, clandestine marriages drag in their train".

Even poor Griffin himself, who was to suffer such torments of conscience about the moral effects of his fiction, might have been a little surprised at this interpretation of his best-known work.

In the critical field, the earliest significant work was done by Thomas Flanagan all of twenty years ago in his pioneering study, *The Irish Novelists 1800-1850.* More recently, Mark Hawthorne has published, in the "Salzburg Studies in English Literature" series, a short but illuminating study of the brothers Banim which bears the suggestive sub-title "A Study in the Early Development of the Anglo-Irish Novel". Flanagan, feeling that he was blazing a new critical trail, clearly believed that he had to demolish some old-fashioned critical assumptions which he considered unhelpful. The two critics to whom he makes reference in this connection are Douglas Hyde and Daniel Corkery. The former had cut through his difficulties in a magisterial fashion, which at least simplified the problem for him, by excluding from consideration in his *Literary History of Ireland* (1899) 'the work of Anglicised Irishmen of the last two centuries'. Hyde was writing the history of 'the literature produced by the Irish-speaking Irish' and was, therefore, justified in his approach by limits he had set himself but Flanagan was quick to point out that 'if Irish culture is to be defined by the Gaelic language, we must conclude that when the last of the hedge-poets died, Ireland ceased to have a culture'. Although he did not find Daniel Corkery's cultural nationalism to his taste either, Flanagan nevertheless felt that Corkery had at least formulated some of the questions which must be raised about the nineteenth century novelists, questions about the relationship between this literature and the people of Ireland:

> Corkery has ... defined somewhat inadvertently the anomalous status of the Irish literature of the nineteenth and twentieth centuries. It is a literature which has never been able to depend for its existence on Irish opinion; only rarely has it been written primarily for its own people; more rarely still has it drawn upon "traits" established in the literature. And yet it is a literature rooted in Irish life and experience, a literature which often forces us to turn for elucidation to the thought and culture of Ireland.

The Irish critical landscape was not, however, quite as barren of congenial critical spirits as Flanagan's introductory chapters might suggest. In view of his important contention that 'a culture must be judged by what it does, not by what it should be doing', Flanagan might have been happier with the judgements of a pioneering Irish critic whose work he does not mention. In *Literature in Ireland: Studies Irish and Anglo-Irish* (1916), Thomas MacDonagh had made a very similar point about the Anglo-Irish writers of both the eighteenth and nineteenth centuries:

> I would not be taken as wishing in any way to belittle the intentions of these writers or of those others mentioned above, who were, as I have said, something out of joint. They lived according to their lights. They did the work they found to their hands.

The spirit of this comment seems close enough to Flanagan's general attitude. MacDonagh focuses his own basic discriminations around the vital issue of language. The opening sentence of what follows indicates his awareness of the need for further serious academic studies of the development of the English language in Ireland and also of the entire Gaelic background:

> In later studies I shall have to deal on the one hand with the character and growth of the English language in Ireland and on the other hand with many aspects of the Gaelic language and literature. Here I wish simply to show, without stating an opinion as to the benefit or the pity of it, that an Anglo-Irish literature of individual value, a literature of worth in English, expressing or interpreting or criticising life in Ireland was possible only when the people whose life was the subject matter spoke the English language and spoke it well, and when Irish writers had attained what may be called the plenary use of the English language—such as had decidedly not been attained by some of the Gaelic writers who wrote occasionally in English also—when, in a word, Irish writers and Irish readers were able to practise and to appreciate the art of English poetry and the art of English prose. When this point had been reached by new writers who were

themselves of the people, the English-speaking Irish people, then this literature appeared and not till then.

This directs our attention straightway to the difficult matter of the linguistic flux of the Irish nineteenth century. In an attempt to clarify MacDonagh's general points, it may be helpful to apply some of them to particular works. Let us ask, for example, whether 'the people whose life was the subject matter' of *The Collegians* 'spoke the English language and spoke it well'. Since, as we shall see later, the social scope of Griffin's novel is ambitiously wide, one presumes that the answer to our question would have to be 'some of them did, at any rate'. What *was* the state of spoken English in the Ireland of 1829, anyhow? And had Griffin (or John Banim or William Carleton ...) attained 'the plenary use of the English language', whatever that rather alarming phrase may mean? Some critics, as we shall see, might well answer that they had not. Donald Davie accuses Gerald Griffin of writing what he calls 'babu's English' in parts of *The Collegians* and Mark Hawthorne finds the early novelists linguistically gauche to a surprising degree:

> The Irish were not accustomed to the English language and were unaware of its subtleties and denotations. While the Englishman used his language with a sense of assurance, the Irish speaker of English lacked verbal security. Even if he had not learned English as a second language, he usually spoke with people who lacked the literacy necessary to refine his solecisms. Thus he had a tendency toward malapropism in his vocabulary and gaelicism in his intonation, syntax, and inflection. Those few who acquired more correct forms of the foreign language still tended to differ widely from the native English speaker in their idioms and pronunciation. As Ireland moved toward becoming an English-speaking nation, the language also underwent change, but in the early nineteenth century it still lacked the history of literary usage that is necessary to produce the assurance of a Jane Austen.

I suppose one might respond to that by suggesting that something more than a 'history of literary usage' was necessary to produce 'the assurance of a Jane Austen'. Centuries of social stability might also have something to do with it. Furthermore, of course, one might be entitled to wonder whether the shades of Goldsmith, Sheridan and Thomas Moore would read Hawthorne's remarks with much satisfaction. Even if we apply his comments to writers like the Banims, who are his particular concern, one might still feel there is in them some element of oversimplification. Both John Banim and Gerald Griffin, for example, worked for long periods in London as practising journalists for the magazines and periodicals of the day, and had little choice but to learn to write a current English idiom. It would be far from difficult to produce examples of such work. Many of Griffin's contributions to the *News of Literature and Fashion* would answer our purposes and one might look also in John Banim's *Revelations of the Dead-Alive*. Their idiomatic unease in their novels is not caused by any lack of ability on their part in the writing of a standard English idiom. It derives, rather, from the tangled situation in which they find themselves as novelists, directing their efforts towards an English-speaking public but trying to give that public a creative insight into a linguistically piebald area.

More importantly, I feel, Hawthorne also neglects to indicate how the best of the early novelists turned their very difficulties in regard to idiom to constructive account by confronting head-on the blending of two idioms and two cultures. In some of their very best comic scenes, Griffin, the Banims and Carleton explored through the tangle of language itself the whole complex muddle of the Anglo-Irish situation and, indeed, most of their later successors in the field did likewise. Somerville and Ross, in their novels and short stories, are intensely alive to the social and cultural implications inherent in the fusion of languages which surrounded them in West Cork in the third quarter of the century. They turn this linguistic ragout to splendid account, making use in the process of English, Irish and Anglo-Irish.

That the writers, when they function in this way, are making a virtue of necessity is certainly the case. The nineteenth century is the period during which the native language of Ireland began to go under to English as the spoken language of large masses of the people. There is no absolute agreement on the statistics of this process but it has been suggested that, at the beginning of the century, two million people still spoke Irish. By mid-century this figure had fallen to about one million and the decline thereafter was rapid. The Irish writer who was directing his work to English readers was necessarily aware that he had to render a regional version of English speech as entertainingly and as clearly as possible. In one sense, this was all to the good. The essential charm of the regional is that it is *not* of the metropolis. It attracts by being different from the standard. On the other hand, it must not be so different as to be dauntingly obscure and off-putting. Thus, many Irish writers found themselves unavoidably burdened with an obligation to explain the meanings of Irish or Anglo-Irish phrases, place-names, customs and so on. The Irish novel of the early part of the century nearly always comes to us with its footnotes or afternotes packed with details of regional explication.

The same historical process which brought about the writers' linguistic difficulties also saw to it that the society which these writers confronted was alarmingly resistant to the conventional forms of the English Novel. Jane Austen might write to her niece in 1814 that '3 or 4 Families in a Country Village is the very thing to work on' but her Irish counterpart could feel no such happy social confidence. An Ireland only just beginning to shake itself free of the worst effects of the Penal Laws and embarking on the tedious struggle for Catholic Emancipation bore little relation to the England of Mr Knightley and Emma Woodhouse. The historian, Edmund Curtis, indicates the menacing mixture of apathy and violence which followed on the Act of Union:

> Under the dull rule of Lord Hardwicke and the Duke of Bedford, Ireland was a very dead country which it was the main aim of government to keep

down by the Convention act, the suspension of Habeas Corpus, and the Coercion acts which make the melancholy story that from 1796 to 1823 only four or five years were of normal civil government. The justification was the simmering of armed revolt following on '98 and the continued agrarian disorder and crimes of the White-boys, 'Shanavests', 'Caravats', and other peasant bodies protesting against tithes, rents, and their other oppressions.

Another modern historian, J. C. Beckett, has also remarked on the sense of national anti-climax in the Ireland of the early 1800s:

> After the excitement and the rapid changes of the later eighteenth century ... the political life of Ireland in the early 1800s seemed drab, and, at least to outward appearance, almost meaningless. Dublin, though it remained the centre of administration and the seat of a vice-regal court, was now little more than a provincial city. One by one the mansions of the nobility were turned over to other purposes; and the parliament house itself was sold to the Bank of Ireland, with the significant stipulation that the interior should be so reconstructed as to efface every visible reminder of its original function.

In 1812, two years before Jane Austen wrote to her niece, Anna, her concept of the novel as indicated above, Maria Edgeworth published *The Absentee*. In that novel, Lord Colambre comes to post-Union Ireland so that Miss Edgeworth may take him and us on the guided tour of Ireland which constitutes the action of the book. Immediately on arrival in Dublin, Colambre is treated to an account of Dublin society as it existed in the years just after the Union. His fictional informant is Sir James Brooke, who works very hard indeed to convince him that, far from ruining Dublin society, the flight of the nobility from the capital after it lost its Parliament had been positively beneficial. Sir James's account is a prosy affair, much too long to quote in full, but, broadly speaking, he argues that when the aristocracy left Ireland, their place was taken by wealthy tradesmen. There followed, according to Sir James, a brief period of social confusion and then, gradually, the nobility, some of them at any rate, came back again, and hey presto, Dublin suddenly found itself possessed of both rank and ability:

> "So that now," concluded Sir James, "you find a society in Dublin composed of a most agreeable and salutary mixture of birth and education, gentility and knowledge, manner and matter; and you see pervading the whole new life and energy, new talent, new ambition, a desire and a determination to improve and be improved—a perception that higher distinction can now be obtained in almost all company, by genius and merit, than by airs and address ...

One cannot help feeling that the lady, through the medium of Sir James, doth protest too much. Her letter of 1834 to her step-brother, Michael Pakenham Edgeworth, in which she formally abandons her Irish fiction, carries a more convincing ring of truth:

It is impossible to draw Ireland as she now is in the book of fiction—realities are too strong, party passions too violent, to bear to see, or care to look at their faces in a looking glass. The people would only break the glass, and curse the fool who held the mirror up to nature—distorted nature, in a fever. We are in too perilous a case to laugh, humour would be out of season, worse than bad taste.

About the same time, her younger contemporaries, Gerald Griffin and the brothers Banim, were confronting the same forbidding Ireland but were proposing to present it fictionally to their English readers in such a way as to exonerate the Irish from the conventional judgements made upon them by an unsympathetic English press. That they were facing formidable difficulties is indicated by the following passage, taken from an article on Irish Novels in the *Edinburgh Review* of February, 1826:

> The advantage of being a *terra incognita,* at least to English statesmen, Ireland has, till lately, possessed almost as fully as the interior of Africa. Even at present, a writer who lays the scene of his story ... in the Hon. Member for Galway's Kingdom of Connemara, is assuredly as safe there from topographical criticism as he would be from the King's writ, and may describe away with as little fear of surveillance or detection as if he were writing ... about Fatteconda or Timbucktoo.

Both John Banim and Gerald Griffin knew all too well, from their years of residence in London, the extent of the English public's ignorance of and indifference to the sister island. In 1823, Griffin, in a letter to his older brother and guardian, Dr William Griffin, gave vent to some rather irritable sentiments not too far removed from those expressed by the writer in the *Edinburgh Review*:

> You have a queer notion on the other side of the water, that your concerns are greatly thought about here. It is a doubt to me if the 'dear little island' were swallowed by a whale, or put in a bag and sent off to the moon, if the circumstance would occasion any further observation than a 'dear me', at one end of the town, and a 'my eyes!' at the other, unless, indeed, among the Irish mining speculators, or some gentlemen equally interested. In all that does not concern their interest or their feelings, these are the most apathetic people breathing.

When he wrote this, Gerald Griffin was living, or barely living, in an unfriendly London where he had yet to make his mark. In Flanagan's revealing description of him he 'moved through London like an Indian scouting hostile territory' and he was to develop a strong and lasting dislike for the great city where he experienced so much lonely misery. At first, he hoped to make a career as a dramatist but, when he failed completely to realise this ambition, he turned to the writing of regional fiction and began to come to grips with the full implications of his efforts to forge a constructive literary role for himself, first as an expatriate Irish writer and subsequently as an Irish writer based in his homeland but seeking an audience outside it. His task was to present the *terra incognita,* with all its linguistic and social turbulence, to English readers and to do this through fictional forms appropriate to the middle-class mores of the larger island. He explained his purpose in the afternote which he appended to the two tales, *The Rivals and Tracy's Ambition* (1829). He first referred to the work done by the Banims:

> The authors who write under the assumed name of the "O'Hara Family", were the first ... who painted the Irish peasant sternly from the life; they placed him before the world in all his ragged energy and cloudy loftiness of spirit, they painted him as he is, goaded by the sense of national and personal wrong, and venting his long pent up agony in the savage cruelty of his actions, in the powerful idiomatic eloquence of his language, in the wild truth and unregulated generosity of his sentiments, in the scalding vehemence of his reproaches, and the shrewd and biting satire of his jests.

He then goes on to indicate how he himself has tried to delineate 'a different order of feelings':

> We have endeavoured in most instances, where pictures of Irish cottage life have been introduced, to furnish a softening corollary to the more exciting moral chronicles of our predecessors, to bring forward the sorrows and the affections more frequently than the violent and fearful passions of the people.

Griffin, then, saw himself as the depictor of the gentler aspects of the violent and troubled Ireland which was put before the English reader by the Banims. In fact, John Banim, in particular, would seem to have moved in a similar direction to Griffin's. Late in 1828, he wrote a long letter to his brother, in which he counsels him:

> No matter from what class of life you take your future materials, seek as much as possible for the good and amiable in our national character and habits; as well as for the strong, the fierce, and I will say the ungovernable.

The letter goes on to detail John's fond memories of various characters he recalls from his youth, including their mother. Concerning all these he assures his brother:

> My dear Michael, if health permitted, I could use these people, and bring their real and unimagined qualities into play, with credit to the Irish character, all Papist as it is, sweetly, primitively, and amiably.

It is this aspect of the fiction which causes Thomas Flanagan to point out that 'the Irish novel, in one of its aspects, can be termed a kind of advocacy before the bar of English public opinion'. The writers often strain to convince English readers of the peaceful nature of the majority of the people of Ireland. Griffin constantly condemns the activities of Whiteboys and other 'night-walkers' though he tries in his best fiction to give some indication of the appalling political mismanagement which brought such violence into being. In 1832, while he was in England researching the material for his historical novel, *The Duke of Monmouth,* he wrote to his beloved Lydia Fisher, at home in Ireland:

14

Oh, dear, Lydia, why didn't you make the Whitefeet (*sic*) behave themselves? They have almost made me ashamed of my country; and general as the outcry is through England at this dreadful law they are making, I am almost tempted to wonder that we have any friends at all, when I hear of one murder after another being committed by these unhappy wretches. But I must not touch on politics; and don't you be offended at my calling you to an account about the Whitefeet.

The impulse to explain the Irish peasants' case, though a worthy one in itself, leads in the fiction to long, inevitably tedious exchanges like those between Abel Tracy and Shanahan in *Tracy's Ambition.* These explicatory prosings are all the more regrettable in view of the vivid dramatisation in the same work of the vile malpractices of Dalton which lead to Tracy's own fierce passion of revenge. The Banims' work also was profoundly affected in a similar manner and, towards the end of his pain-racked life, the ailing John vetoed a proposal from Michael that they should collaborate on yet another tale of agrarian violence similar to the sort of work they had done earlier in tales such as *Crohoore of the Billhook* and *The Croppy.* John's biographer, Patrick Murray, provides Michael's account of this decision:

> I had, some time before, filled a note-book with materials referrable to the latest agrarian confederacy, that had disturbed our neighbourhood, the actors in which had bestowed on themselves the fantastical name of 'Whitefeet'. With some of the principal leaders of this lawless and widespread combination I had held intercourse; I had gained a knowledge of their signs and passwords, and obtained an insight into their views and proceedings. I proposed a tale wherein my materials could be used; my adviser differed with me.
>
> "We have given," he said, "perhaps too much of the dark side of the Irish character; let us, for the present, treat of the amiable; enough of it is around us."

In the event, they embarked together on *Father Connell,* a study of a kindly old parish priest recalled from boyhood memories, a work of pious celebration rather than a realistic exploration of their society. There is an echo here of Maria Edgeworth's earlier renunciation of unduly violent Irish themes.

Griffin died young, in 1840, and Banim, who had been grievously ill for many years, followed him in 1842. A few years later came the fearsome climax of all the social ills and political mismanagements of the first half of the century, the Great Hunger, the potato famine which forms the century's watershed after which nothing was to be quite the same again. Of the native Irish novelists, Carleton was the only one to survive it and he was to describe himself as *ultimus Romanorum,* once Griffin and John Banim were gone. Thomas Davis died in 1845, Daniel O'Connell in 1847. John Mitchel was transported in 1848 and the damp squib of the abortive Rising of the same year fizzled out with the transportation of Smith O'Brien and Thomas Francis Meagher. The impulse of the Young Ireland movement which had once seemed so vigorous had for the moment come to an end in a country where the mere business of staying alive left little time for any other activity, political or literary. The sombre and terrible mood of this period is powerfully conveyed in Carleton's *The Black Prophet*. Irish politics now began to move into the area of organised agrarian agitation designed to win back the land for the Irish people. A decade later came the brief, mismanaged Fenian insurrection of 1867 which threw up one notable Irish writer, Charles Kickham, of whom Yeats wrote with interest and respect. Kickham is often compared with Carleton, perhaps because there is a tendency to feel that both writers were addressing themselves to the Irish people rather than to the English audience envisaged by Edgeworth, Griffin and the Banims. In fact, as we shall see, Kickham's work was conditioned by pressures similar to those which had shaped the work of the earlier novelists and Carleton, as Flanagan points out, attached to his collected stories a preface 'in which the author acknowledged the English reading public as his probable audience'.

As the century advanced, the 'Big House' fiction, in the hands of its finest exponents, began to reflect the declining fortunes of the Ascendancy. The purposeful optimism which Maria Edgeworth so bravely voiced about post-Union Ireland rings hollow against the background of Land League agitiation and peasant violence which forms the ground bass for George Moore's *A Drama in Muslin*. The last novel considered here, Somerville and Ross's *The Real Charlotte,* is a vivid and poignant evocation of what Conor Cruise O'Brien has called 'the Indian Summer of the Ascendancy'. Both Moore's novel and that of Somerville and Ross, in their different ways, vividly evoke the Ireland of their time and both are in a very real sense elegiac in tone. These novels, and others of their ilk, convey to us the powerful imaginative insights of a ruling class from which power was fast slipping away as they finally lost their hold on the land which they had held by right of conquest for several centuries. The work of the native novelists gives us glimpses of the lives of those who existed outside the Ascendancy laager. We are back with the Yeatsian definition with which we began but have come to see, perhaps, that the novelist with a gentry accent and the novelist with a peasant accent had a great deal in common. They inhabited the same troubled land, they both had to court a foreign audience. Their points of view in relation to their material may have been radically different but their technical problems in regard to form and language and the devising of a creative idiom were a burden common to both.

The nineteenth century saw Ireland change its language and its rulers. An oppressed people began to assert themselves, while their traditional oppressors gave ground slowly and reluctantly. Everything is in flux, language, political power, ownership of land. The sort of social stability favourable to the well-upholstered, realistic, English middle-class novel does not exist. And so, again and again, the writers' materials prove intractable in relation to the form adopted. The impressive sexual frankness of Banim's *The*

Nowlans lapses into conventional melodrama. Griffin's strange, hysterical hero, Hardress Cregan, gropes towards an explanation of his contradictions and wallows in oceans of fustian. Even Carleton, greatest of them all, cannot find a truly expressive fictional shape for the huge anger which fills him in the presence of national calamity. As Flanagan, who has responded to the fiction of the period with unusual imaginative sympathy and power, has it:

> The history of the Irish novel is one of continuous attempts to represent the Irish experience within conventions which were not innately congenial to it. Maria Edgeworth's novels-with-thesis, Lady Morgan's exotic romances, Gerald Griffin's moralities, the picaresque narratives of William Carleton are all encumbered in certain essential ways by the conventions which they have assumed. The best of them, which seek to move beyond these forms, make their strongest points and exist most vividly through indirection, symbol, allusion, and subtle shifts of points of view.

Flanagan would also have it that 'the nineteenth-century Irish novel established no tradition', seeming to feel that the literary impulse collapsed at mid-century:

> Yeats was to write, "We and our bitterness have left no traces/On Munster grass and Connemara skies". But the bitterness still lived in the Irish air, and was bred in the Irish bone. The grass, the skies, the rivers and towers served the early novelists as double emblems of hatred and love. Each writer was driven into despairing silence only when the possibility of meaningful choice was removed. ... In the years which followed 1850, the despair was universal. To have supposed during those decades that Ireland possessed the ability to choose its own destiny would have been to indulge the conjectures of sentimentalists or fanatics. And it was in those decades that the tradition of the Irish novel withered.

This assertion has, in modern times, been clearly contradicted by one group of novels at least, those stemming from the 'Big-House' tradition which is represented in the present work by. *Castle Rackrent, A Drama in Muslin* and *The Real Charlotte*. In recent years, this kind of novel has had a late blossoming of an amazing kind. The imagination of modern Ireland, for so long concerned with the period following on the achievement of some sort of national independence of the old enemy, seems recently to have felt the need for a kind of adjustment of the national psyche, as the century entered its second half. At any rate, whatever the reason, there has recently been a spate of fine novels which have derived their force from a concern with the tag-end of a gentry tradition which might have seemed to have long since had its day. Aidan Higgins, Jennifer Johnston, John Banville, J. G. Farrell, Helen Wykham, Caroline Blackwood, have all produced novels which have won deserved acclaim, not merely from an Irish audience. Historical nostalgia can be only part of the explanation of this phenomenon. The best of these novels, works like *Troubles* or *Langrishe Go Down* or *The Captains and the Kings,* have undoubtedly achieved, quite independently of their historical revaluation, a genuine relevance to certain contemporary preoccupations of modern man. The Langrishe sisters, fatally separated from their parents' past, founder into a Beckettian solipsism. Jennifer Johnston's Mr Prendergast is not just a piece of Anglo-Irish flotsam—he is also a man stripped of the traditional beliefs of his class, desperately searching for love in a darkening universe. Who would have thought the old *genre* would have so much blood in it! How extraordinary it was to see Caroline Blackwood gain a well-deserved nomination for the Booker Prize with the Ulster version of *Castle Rackrent, Great Granny Webster* (1977)!

In other areas also, one feels, the tradition may not be quite as broken as Flanagan would have us believe. Modern novels may not indulge in the gothic swoonings and contrivances into which, at their weakest, the nineteenth century novels tend to lapse, but the occasional, powerful realities of the early novels surely speak to our modern curiosities and concerns? Banim's John Nowlan is not entirely unrelated to the young Mahoney of John McGahern's *The Dark*. Both are fierce perfectionists tortured by their lustful natures. Kickham's country folk have their counterparts in the fiction of Corkery or Kavanagh. The vigorous verbal comedy of a Joyce or a Flann O'Brien must surely owe something to the linguistic pyrotechnics of Carleton's philomaths. Tonally, thematically, linguistically, topographically, contemporary Irish fiction constantly confesses its debt to the past. As one reads the stories of Griffin and Carleton and Banim, one finds in them the ordinary people of Ireland, being presented fictionally for the first time in English. These stories, as Yeats says, are 'Ireland talking to herself'. The eavesdropper is often richly rewarded.

I

Maria Edgeworth
CASTLE RACKRENT

Maria Edgeworth 1768-1849

Maria Edgeworth's date of birth used to be given as 1 January 1767 but she herself seems to have considered 1768 correct and her latest biographer, Marilyn Butler, concurs. There is no doubt about her place of birth, Black Bourton in Oxfordshire. Her father, Richard Lovell Edgeworth, was the second son of an Anglo-Irish landowner. Richard Lovell inherited his father's property in 1770, his elder brother having died in childhood. All those who have written about Maria have inevitably found themselves writing also about her idiosyncratic and interesting father, with whose long career her own is so inextricably woven. To give Richard Lovell the sort of training which would fit him for his duties as a landowner, his father sent him at the age of sixteen in 1760 to Trinity College, Dublin, but he did little there apart from drinking and gambling. In the following year his father despatched him to Oxford, to live at the house of a friend, Paul Elers, and to enrol as an undergraduate at Corpus Christi College. The amorous young Irishman soon became involved with Elers' eldest daughter, Anna Maria, and eloped with her to Scotland in 1763. When the couple returned to Black Bourton the following year, Richard Edgeworth reluctantly accepted the situation and had the couple legally remarried at Black Bourton. In spite of the romantic circumstances of their union, the pair were never very happy together. He found her lacking in the social graces, almost illiterate and given to constant complainings but, before her early death in 1773, she had presented him with five children of whom four survived. Maria was the third in order of birth and the first girl.

It was during the period of this first of his four marriages that Richard Lovell encountered for the first time a group of intelligent and inventive friends with whom he was to remain in touch for many years. Among these was Thomas Day, a fervent disciple of the educational theories of Rousseau, whose engaging eccentricities far surpassed those of Richard Lovell himself. Others were Erasmus Darwin; Josiah Wedgwood, the potter; James Watt, the engineer and James Keir, an industrial chemist. These men were members of a scientific group known as the Lunar Circle and Edgeworth was introduced into this society in 1766. They shared a common interest in the application of science to the problems of industry and Richard Lovell's lively and inventive mind fitted him admirably for membership. He had a consuming interest in machinery of all kinds, in the invention of a working telegraph system, in the building of roads and canals, the making of carriages and other types of transportation. Many considered him a crank and an oddity but it may have been the very range of his multifarious interests which earned him this reputation. He was, in fact, quick-witted and creative and might have been taken more seriously by his contemporaries if he had narrowed the range of his interests and pursued one of them to an entirely successful conclusion.

Maria's mother died in 1773, giving birth to a daughter, Anna, and Richard Lovell married Honora Sneyd later in the same year. Maria was now about five years old and seems to have spent a rather lonely childhood. She later recalled that her mother 'was always crying' and she found her new stepmother rather cold and distant. The child paid her first visit to Ireland in 1773 when her father, with his new bride, was forced to return to his Irish estate by financial pressures. Two years later, the young Maria was sent to school at Derby, to a Mrs Latuffiere who seems to have treated the girl kindly. She was happy at the school and retained pleasant memories of her teachers in later life. In 1777, Richard and Honora moved back to England and the young Maria could then spend her holidays with them at the new home in Northchurch in Hertfordshire. Honora died of tuberculosis in 1780 and Richard Lovell married her sister, Elisabeth Sneyd, later the same year, a course of action which Honora herself had urged upon him before her death. Maria left her school in Derby in 1781 and went briefly to a more fashionable establishment run by a Mrs Devis at Upper Wimpole Street, London.

In the following year, her father made the move which was to decide the future novelist's entire career. In 1782, Richard Lovell decided that the time had come for him to cease being an absentee landlord and he and his new wife, with the children of his earlier marriages, settled at Edgeworthstown, where Maria was to spent the rest of her long and active life. She was now fifteen, old enough to have formed some views about life, young enough to absorb fresh and vivid impressions of her new and strange environment. She was utterly devoted to her father and seems to have given up her life in England quite happily, in the belief that she would come closer to her father by sharing in his work in Ireland. This she did, collaborating with him in many enterprises, including the education of his large and growing family, until his death in 1817, by which time Maria herself was almost fifty. All her biographers, and they have been many, have had to tackle the vexed question of the extent and nature of Richard Lovell Edgeworth's influence on his celebrated daughter and on her works. At one time it was customary to blame him entirely for the strongly didactic element which pervades the great bulk of her published work but this version of their relationship was exposed as an oversimplification by Roger McHugh as long ago as 1938 in a discerning article in *Studies*. It is there pointed out that 'the taste of the time and of her father, and the current of ethical, economic and humanitarian thought which the French Revolution set flowing in English literature, had much to say to this, but it is probable that her own experience as a teacher had even more, and that her didacticism continued a matter of choice'. Marilyn Butler, in her recent biography, also opposes the older view of the father as a pernicious influence on the daughter and argues instead that the truth is quite other. She provides much interesting information from letters and other documents to support her contentions.

At any rate, we know that from the time they settled in Ireland, Maria and her father were involved together in all the business of the estate and that she became a sort of permanent secretary to him, riding out with him to visit tenants, being present with him at the settling of disputes, the payment of rents and all the varied business of a prosperous Protestant Ascendancy landlord. This gave her an opportunity to observe his enlightened improvements to his estate and to get to know at first hand the ordinary Irish people who were to form an important part of her literary material. Her earliest writings were of a specifically didactic nature, since they were stories devised for the education of her own brothers and sisters. These were first written down on a slate and were not put on paper until they had been approved by the family itself. Thus, her early efforts at story-telling constitute an example of her enlightened approach to the education of the young and also of her creative humility and willingness to submit her work to the intensely practical criticism of others. In this way she produced *The Parent's Assistant* in 1796 and, in 1798, she collaborated with her father in a work entitled *Practical Education,* thereby bringing to completion an enterprise on which Richard Lovell had first embarked with his beloved Honora some years earlier.

In the same year of 1798, a desperately troubled one for Ireland, Richard Lovell married his fourth wife, Frances Anne Beaufort, who was a year younger than his daughter, Maria. Happily, Maria and her latest stepmother got on very well together from the beginning and the new marriage did not disrupt Maria's close relationship with her father. She usually submitted her work for his approval but, in one celebrated instance, she broke this rule. She wrote her most famous novel, her first one, *Castle Rackrent,* without him and subsequently refused to alter or extend it at his request. It appeared in 1800, the year in which Ireland lost its Protestant Ascendancy Parliament and was joined in the Union with Great Britain. Both Maria and her father firmly believed that Ireland's welfare would be advanced by the Union but, characteristically, he voted against the measure because of his intense disapproval of the corrupt methods employed to bring it about.

One of Maria's best-known novels of manners, *Belinda,* appeared in 1801 and in the following year she accompanied her parents on a trip to England and France, during which she met many of the leading intellectuals of the day. It was on this trip that Maria had her one and only proposal of marriage, from a Swedish gentleman, the Chevalier Edelcrantz. She turned him down because she was reluctant to leave her family and her home for a distant land, but she seems to have gone on thinking seriously about him for some time afterwards. In 1809 she publised the first set of her *Tales of Fashionable Life,* which included her second Irish novel, *Ennui.* The second set of these *Tales,* which included *The Absentee,* appeared in 1812. The last of her specifically Irish novels, *Ormond,* appeared at the time of her father's death, in 1817. She was profoundly affected by his passing and by the sundering of their long partnership. She was to survive him by over thirty years, living on into the terrible years of the Great Hunger, during which she worked tirelessly for the relief of her people in the Edgeworthstown area.

Her active literary life lies between the Union and the Famine and she gradually came to feel that she could no longer bear to write about Ireland. The rational optimism which she shared with her father in their early years in Ireland, their liberal and enlightened plans for non-sectarian schools and benevolent improvement of their tenants' lot, all these were swamped by the dark tide of hunger and violence which deluged Ireland at mid-century. After her father's death, she obeyed his request by editing his *Memoirs* in 1820. She paid several visits to England and, in 1823, called on Sir Walter Scott at Edinburgh and later stayed with him at Abbotsford. Scott returned the visit in 1825. In the same year in which the *Memoirs* were published, 1820, she returned to France and travelled also in Switzerland. She was received everywhere with honour and acclaim. Her last novel, *Helen,* was published in 1834. Her last published work was *Orlandino* in 1848, the profits from which went to raise money for the victims of the Famine. She died on 22 May, 1849.

CASTLE RACKRENT

> We hear from very good authority that the king was much pleased with
> *Castle Rackrent*—he rubbed his hands and said, 'What what—I know
> something now of my Irish subjects.'

So wrote Richard Lovell Edgeworth to his father-in-law, Daniel Augustus
Beaufort, in April 1800, a few short months after the first, anonymous
appearance of the novel. The modern reader, bemused by a wide variety of
responses to the work, must admire the royal confidence and speculate mildly
as to what exactly George III may have thought he had learned about his Irish
subjects from this first and most celebrated of Maria Edgeworth's many
novels. The book is, of course, an important landmark in the history of the
English novel and a seminal work in the Anglo-Irish tradition of 'Big-House'
fiction. Walter Allen, in *The English Novel,* concurs with P. H. Newby's
striking claim that 'whereas Jane Austen was so much the better novelist
Maria Edgeworth may be the more important' and proceeds to indicate how
the tiny Anglo-Irish spinster extended the form:

> Miss Edgeworth occupied new territory for the novel. Before her, except
> when London was the scene, the locale of our fiction had been
> generalized, conventionalized. Outside London and Bath, the
> eighteenth-century novelist rarely had a sense of place; the background of
> his fiction is as bare of scenery almost as an Elizabethan play; and when
> landscape came in for its own sake, with Mrs Radcliffe, it was there not
> because it was a specific landscape but because it was a romantic one.
> Maria Edgeworth gave fiction a local habitation and a name. And she did
> more than this: she perceived the relation between the local habitation
> and the people who dwell in it. She invented, in other words, the regional
> novel, in which the very nature of the novelist's characters is conditioned,
> receives its bias and expression, from the fact that they live in a
> countryside differentiated by a traditional way of life from other
> countryside.

Allen goes on to recount Scott's celebrated tribute to the Irish novelist in the
postscript to *Waverley,* where Scott declared that his aim in fiction was 'in
some distant degree to emulate the admirable Irish portraits drawn by Miss
Edgeworth' and the equally celebrated link with Turgenev, on which recent
scholarship has cast a more sceptical eye. Whatever about Turgenev, though,
there is no doubt that in *Castle Rackrent* Maria Edgeworth produced the first
significant regional novel and the first striking example of a saga novel which
traces the history of a family through several generations. In the presence of
all that historical significance it is a positive relief to remind oneself that it all
began with a young girl imitating one of her father's workmen. How right it is,
somehow, that this important little work should have originated with its
author's absorption in a particular kind of dialogue. The Anglo-Irish novel,
quite properly, begins with good talk.

Like Edith Somerville and Violet Martin later in the century, Maria revelled in the emergent Anglo-Irish of the ordinary people. She listened with delight to the talk of her father's tenants, as she rode with him around his estate at Edgeworthstown. She learned from her father the habit of collecting curious habits of speech and striking turns of phrase and often entertained the family by mimicking her father's steward, John Langan. In one of her letters she indicated how familiar she became with this figure:

> The only character drawn from life in 'Castle Rackrent' is Thady himself, the teller of the story. He was an old steward (not very old, though, at the time; I added to his age, to allow him time for the generations of the family). I heard him when I first came to Ireland, and his dialect struck me, and his character; and I became so acquainted with it, that I could think and speak in it without effort, so that when, for mere amusement, without any idea of publishing, I began to write a family history as Thady would tell it, he seemed to stand beside me and dictate; and I wrote as fast as my pen could go ... .

Her aunt, Mrs Ruxton, urged her to write down her mimicry and so she devised the tale of the first three Rackrent squires. The later part of the novel, concerning Sir Condy Rackrent, was added some two years later.

Thus, she began with Thady Quirk and he has continued to be the heart of the matter ever since. In making him her narrator and controller of the novel's point of view, she established a new technique of fiction and presented commentators with a cat's-cradle of speculation about her central figure and the relationship between him and his material. Critical diagnosis has run the gamut from the innocent Thady to the malign Thady. To some he has seemed the devoted and innocuous servitor, to others the scheming *agent provocateur*. G. H. Gerould, in *The Patterns of English and American Fiction,* informs us that 'Thady Quirk was made to tell us in his own simpleminded and confused way how the Rackrent family came to ruin'. A. N. Jeffares, in an Introduction to a 1953 edition of three stories by Maria Edgeworth (*Castle Rackrent, Emilie de Coulanges* and *The Birthday Present*), skates skilfully around and past the problem with the announcement that 'the art of Maria disappears in the artlessness of Thady, and, one might add, the artfulness of his son, Jason, who is left largely and cleverly to the reader's imagination'. Since the critical task is, presumably, to assess the nature and degree of Maria's art, this critical *glissade* hardly takes us much further. A more useful gloss is supplied by Thomas Flanagan who finds the novel's 'acts and statements ambiguous and unsettling' and comes to grips with the problem of Thady in a much more forthright manner:

> It purports to be an account, dictated by an illiterate servant named Thady M'Quirk (sic), of the fortunes of four generations of the Rackrent family, which has ceased to exist in name, though not, perhaps, in blood. Thady is a partisan of the family, or rather, of "the honor of the family". Only when the story is finished does the reader realize that Thady has his own wry view of the matter. But, even so, he does not fully understand the

story which he is telling. The meaning and passion with which he instinctively invests the words "honor" and "loyalty" lead him to bring forth evidence which prompts the reader to a quite different judgement of the Rackrents.

George Watson, in his detailed and useful Introduction to his 1964 edition of the novel in the Oxford English Novels series, asserts that 'the telling reality of *Rackrent,* of course, lies in the narrator-figure of Old Thady himself, and the device is so expertly used as to make us wonder why Maria Edgeworth never used it again'. He also comments that 'this large device of irony gives *Rackrent* a coherence which no other of Miss Edgeworth's novels achieves, and one which fully compensates for an episodic design'. Unfortunately, he does not probe the figure of Thady very deeply on his own account and, once again, one is left with the slightly frustrated feeling that mere assertion of the novel's 'coherence', in the presence of so many conflicting critical responses, is hardly going to the heart of the matter. It was left to James Newcomer, in his 1967 bicentennial study, *Maria Edgeworth the Novelist,* to formulate the clearest and most specific version of the 'malign' Thady. Newcomer, in a chapter which concentrates on the isolation of those points in the work where Thady's actions or omissions conduce most fully to the advancement of his son, Jason, and to the ruin of the Rackrents, enters a solid indictment against Thady:

> The Thady whom we now recognize is a more important creation than Thady the unreflecting servant. Far from being simple, he is relatively complex. The true Thady reflects intellect and power in the afflicted Irish peasant, who in generations to come will revolt and revolt again. He is artful rather than artless, unsentimental rather than sentimental, shrewd rather than obtuse, clear-headed rather than confused, calculating rather than trusting. There is less affection in our view of the true Thady, but now we have to feel a degree of admiration for him.

There, then, we have it: the ingenuous Thady; the Thady who 'does not fully understand the story he is telling'; the crafty and calculating Thady and the Thady who is the vengeful representative of a dispossessed people. The commentators agree on Thady's central importance but they agree on little else. Miss Edgeworth would seem to have had the rights of it, indeed, when she wrote that Thady 'seemed to stand beside me and dictate'.

In the presence of so many conflicting opinions, let us go first to the writer herself, turning our backs firmly on Messrs Wimsatt and Beardsley and all the dreadful hazards of intentionalism. Their dire warning that 'critical inquiries are not settled by consulting the oracle' was, after all, directed to readers of poetry rather than to that more casual and impure form, the novel. So, what sort of novel did Maria Edgeworth herself believe she was writing? Let us first remind ourselves that *Castle Rackrent* was her first novel and that she never again wrote another quite like it. Then, also, we should remember that all her previous writings had been of a specifically didactic and educational nature and, indeed, as Marilyn Butler often indicates in her biography, Maria herself seemed to feel that the Edgeworthian contribution to educational theory was of much more significance than her fiction. She often gives the firm impression that she believed the world would attend more eagerly to her own and her father's works on education than to her fictions. *Pace* Wimsatt and Beardsley again, *Castle Rackrent* appears to have come about almost by accident, almost (dare one say?) for fun.

It is also, surely, important that it was not written all at once, but in two clearly separate parts, the second achieved two years after the first so that if we are being rash enough to try to probe the writer's intentions, we must allow that her views may have changed in that long period of composition and that the design of the book, short as it is, may not be conveniently all of a piece. Sir Condy Rackrent may call for different responses from those we bring to bear on his crazy predecessors. The sub-title of the novel is 'An Hibernian Tale taken from facts and from the manners of the Irish squires before the year 1782'. Maria had, of course, arrived in Ireland in that same heady year of 1782, the first year of the Irish Independency, of 'Grattan's Parliament' which had promised so much and passed out of existence after less than two decades. Maria is, therefore, indicating firmly that the events of her novel belong to the past. The Irish squires of her story, she is telling us, are old-fashioned, outdated figures, not at all representative of the Anglo-Irish upper classes of the present time (i.e. the turn of the century). In 1800, the terrible events of the '98 Rising were a mere two years in the past. The Edgeworths' hazardous situation in relation to their loyal fellow-Protestants had been evidenced by the attacks on Richard Lovell Edgeworth after the defeat of the French invaders and Maria would certainly not have wished to cause renewed offence by any suggestion that the rackety squireens of her novel were in any way representative of her own class at the time of the Act of Union. *Castle Rackrent,* we are to understand, is an account of a by-gone age and of figures safely distanced from us by time. It is this which leads George Watson to comment:

> It is difficult for us now, with our knowledge of the Famine and the growth of nationalism, to conceive of the confidence with which the Anglo-Irish governed Ireland in the last years of the eighteenth century. *Rackrent* is a novel of optimism: it is about a bad old day that is dead and gone, however much may remain to be done. Maria's literary career belongs to this world of confident Protestant leadership.

Since Maria's literary career was to continue until after the Famine, we must assume that Watson is referring here only to the early phase of her career. 'Confident Protestant leadership' was certainly long gone by the time she died in 1849. Her own confession of her inability to write further about an Ireland which had passed her by dates from 1834. Apart from all that, however, can we easily accept the notion that *'Rackrent* is a novel of optimism', even if we probe no further than the immediate historical circumstances at the time of its production? If we examine Maria Edgeworth's

Preface and postscript to the novel, I think we may find them a little less than confidently optimistic. The Preface is less helpful here than the postscript, though it will be of much greater relevance when we come to probe the art of the novel itself more fully. For the moment, only the concluding remarks in the Preface are germane to our purposes and they are, in their way, very revealing of Maria Edgeworth's views about her adopted country. Twice in the three short paragraphs which conclude the Preface she refers to national 'identity':

> Nations as well as individuals gradually lose attachment to their identity, and the present generation is amused rather than offended by the ridicule that is thrown upon their ancestors.
>   Probably we shall soon have it in our power, in a hundred instances, to verify the truth of these observations. When Ireland loses her identity by an union with Great Britain, she will look back with a smile of good-humoured complacency on the Sir Kits and Sir Condys of her former existence.

The Ireland about whose identity she is writing so confidently here is clearly the Ireland of the Anglo-Irish Protestant Ascendancy, the 'Irish Protestant Nation' which sold itself for a mess of peerages to Pitt at the time of the Union. Maria Edgeworth's argument here is almost blatantly self-contradictory. On the one hand, she roundly exposes the misdoings of an older generation and, on the other, consoles her contemporaries strangely with the suggetion that their loss of national identity will produce in them a smug, satisfied, amiable 'complacency' which will permit them to look back on their disreputable ancestors with a newly achieved condescension from their standpoint as members of a united kingdom of Great Britain and Ireland. She comes very close here to equating the 'identity' of the Protestant Nation with her Rackrents. The point is not by any means irrelevant to a novel with contradictions at its heart. The Preface also sorts oddly with the postscript, particularly with its conclusion:

> It is a problem of difficult solution to determine, whether an Union will hasten or retard the amelioration of this country. The few gentlemen of education who now reside in this country will resort to England: they are few, but they are in nothing inferior to men of the same rank in Great Britain. The best that can happen will be the introduction of British manufacturers in their places.
>   Did the Warwickshire militia, who were chiefly artisans, teach the Irish to drink beer, or did they learn from the Irish to drink whiskey?

No great confidence about the future there, one feels! She clearly indicates that a dark question-mark hangs over Ireland's immediate future. She makes no reference here, as she did in the Preface, to 'a hundred instances' which will verify predictions of new confidence. She is woundingly frank about the inevitability of the flight of the gentry after the Union and she suggests, with surprising lack of tact, that the men of real education among them are, in any case, few.

A decade later, in Chapter VI of *The Absentee,* she was to try to convince her readers that the society of post-Union Dublin was an improvement on what had gone before. Some of this purposeful whistling in the dark is quoted in the Introduction to the present work. The tone of the postscript to *Castle Rackrent,* however, strikes one as peculiarly despondent and almost fearful. 'The best that can happen,' she says, 'will be the introduction of British manufacturers in their places' and she seems to imply no delight at this prospect. Quite what one is to make of her strange concluding conundrum about the Warwickshire militia is difficult to say. Visitors to Ireland who linger in the country long enough traditionally become 'more Irish than the Irish themselves'. Beer-drinking seems to suggest a sort of lower-class drabness and respectability, almost a kind of flatness. Whiskey-drinking, on the other hand, connotes high spirits. English dullness and Irish flair? Some pious hope, perhaps, that the British manufacturers who will replace the departed lordlings may acquire some Irish *brio* to redeem their native phlegm? In any case, through it all seems to run a profound contempt for the Anglo-Irish squirearchy, which somehow contradicts her earnest assurances about the Rackrents' contemporary irrelevance. Traditionally, after all, it is rats who desert sinking ships. We may feel entitled to conclude that the frankly editorial Preface and postscript are not, in essence, so very different in tone from the matter of the tale itself.

The Preface generally is the best possible starting-point for entry into the story proper. In it Maria Edgeworth enters a modest but firm claim for the vital importance of fiction as opposed to history. Her formulation of her case is full of tantalisingly appropriate hints. We cannot judge men, she tells us, by their public appearance. We must attend, rather, to 'their careless conversations, their half-finished sentences'. Thady looms there already, and she now embarks upon a carefully calculated justification of her choice of Thady as her narrator. In a passage of great elegance she boldly contends that 'the merits of a biographer are inversely as the extent of his intellectual powers and of his literary talents'. Furthermore, 'where we see that a man has the power, we may naturally suspect that he has the will to deceive us', so we can feel real confidence in an unlettered narrator since we can 'see and despise vulgar errors' so are unlikely to be taken in by such a story-teller. The whole passage bristles with calculated innuendo and is written entirely tongue-in-cheek. Nothing could be clearer than that this 'plain unvarnished tale' will indeed be 'the most highly ornamented narrative'. When we put beside this the revealing passage in the postscript which indicates that the details of her story are 'characteristic of that mixture of quickness, simplicity, cunning, carelessness, dissipation, disinterestedness, shrewdness and blunder, which in different forms, and with varying success, has been brought upon the stage or delineated in novels', we must recognize that we are being offered a most carefully calculated piece of literary artifice and that *Castle Rackrent* is an intensely self-conscious piece of subtle fictional contriving.

Most commentators have remarked how the opening of the story constitutes a microcosm of the fortunes of the Rackrents, with Thady indicating the progressive decline through the series of names assigned to him, moving from his 'real' name of Thady Quirk to 'honest Thady', to 'old Thady', and finally to 'poor Thady'. What has been less often remarked is the speed with which Thady is made to draw his son, Jason, into the story, in a curious mixture of pride and disenchantment which, from the very beginning, strikes the note of their intriguing relationship:

> .... to look at me, you would hardly think 'poor Thady' was the father of attorney Quirk; he is a high gentleman, and never minds what poor Thady says, and having better than 1500 a-year, landed estate, looks down upon honest Thady, but I wash my hands of his doings, and as I have lived so will I die, true and loyal to the family.

The family is now, of course, over and done with, so Thady's 'loyalty' can only be to their memory, since the whole novel is a retrospect. Jason is now the established possessor of the estate and Thady, like some reach-me-down Lear, disowns him before launching into his account of the family. Maria Edgeworth makes much play, in the Preface, with the oddity of Thady's language, indicating there that notes have been added to assist 'the *ignorant* English reader' and that 'the editor' had once considered translating the language of Thady into 'plain English' but had decided that 'Thady's idiom is incapable of translation'. All this would seem to suggest that the idiom is very strange indeed. It is, of course, nothing of the kind. Of all celebrated Irish fictional characters, Thady is the least brogue-ridden. What he does possess, however, is a talent for sustained monologue which might be the envy of even one of Samuel Beckett's solipsistic soloists. He also appears to possess an impressive familiarity with a wide range of technical terminology in relation to the business of land-holding and the law. The 'Irishness' of his dialogue is unmistakeable but remarkably discreet in its way, often indicating itself principally by a free use of participles in linked clauses of which many are run together. The tone of the narrative is established with remarkable ease and speed and never flags, seeming thereby to bear out the writer's account of her familiarity with the speech of her father's steward and her facility in mimicking him.

Almost the first thing we learn from Thady about his masters is that the original name of the family was O'Shaughlin and that they were 'related to the kings of Ireland'. Sir Patrick Rackrent, first of the set of four doomed Rackrents we shall be meeting, inherits the estate from Sir Tallyhoo Rackrent. The manner of this inheritance is of some importance and Thady's account of it is almost his first piece of significant smudging of detail:

> My grandfather was driver to the great Sir Patrick O'Shaughlin, and I heard him, when I was a boy, telling how the Castle Rackrent estate came to Sir Patrick—Sir Tallyhoo Rackrent was cousin-german to him, and had a fine estate of his own, only never a gate upon it, it being his maxim,

that a car was the best gate.—Poor gentleman! He lost a fine hunter and
his life, at last, by it, all in one day's hunt.—But I ought to bless that day,
for the estate came straight into *the* family, upon one condition, which Sir
Patrick O'Shaughlin at the time took sadly to heart, they say, but thought
better of it afterwards, seeing how large a stake depended upon it, that he
should, by Act of Parliament, take and bear the sirname and arms of
Rackrent.

Thomas Flanagan is in no doubt about the precise significance of this
passage:

Thady would have us believe that this reluctance issues from Sir Patrick's
knowledge that the O'Shaughlins are 'sons of the kings of Ireland'. Some
of the puzzles of the novel are resolved, however, if we regard this as one
of his discretions. It is more likely that Patrick has had to change not
merely his name but his creed, which would have seemed to the old
Catholic servant the deepest dishonour.

History, of which Maria Edgeworth was an avid reader, would certainly
require us to believe that the Rackrents are Protestants. The story belongs, we
have been told, to the days before 1782. It belongs, therefore, in the period of
the Penal Laws, which bore heavily on Catholics in every way but most
heavily of all, perhaps, in the matter of inheritance of property. Some
wealthy Catholic families conformed to the rival religion in an attempt to
hold on to their property. Many lost their lands through refusing to conform.
There is even a thematic appropriateness about accepting Flanagan's reading
here, since it sets the Rackrents off on their demented careers in a suitable
atmosphere of spiritual cynicism and infidelity. Their distinctive
irresponsibility begins here. In eighteenth-century Ireland, those who
changed their religion for profit were known quite simply as 'perverts' and
since the whole tale of the Rackrents' misdeeds centres on repeated reversals
of their proper role, it seems acceptable that they begin by renouncing what
they ought to have held most dear. There have, however, been other
interpretations of this crucial issue.

In an interesting paper submitted to the I.A.S.A.I.L. conference held at
University College Galway in the summer of 1976, Mr Maurice Colgan of the
University of Bradford argued that the Rackrents are, in fact, Catholics and
that this involves Maria Edgeworth in a significant flight from the historical
facts of her period. Mr Colgan picked out a number of references in the novel
which appeared to support this suggestion. He adverted, for example, to the
point in the narrative where a maid is punished for breaking the Lenten fast
and we are told that Sir Murtagh Rackrent 'never fasted, not he'. This, Mr
Colgan argues, suggests that Sir Murtagh is a slack Catholic, not a
Protestant. The argument, one feels, is hardly conclusive and Mr Colgan
might have appealed more effectively to the slightly earlier part of the
narrative where we are told of Sir Murtagh's wife, the stingy Skinflint widow,
that 'she was a strict observer for self and servants of Lent, and all Fast days,

but not holidays'. This would seem to suggest that Sir Murtagh's wife is herself a Catholic but, even if she is, Sir Murtagh could still be a Protestant. After all, Sir Kit Rackrent later marries a Jew. The Rackrents characteristically marry for mercenary rather than spiritual motives.

Mr Colgan further notes that, in the period in question, it would have been impossible for Jason Quirk, as a Catholic, to enter the legal profession until after Langrishe's Relief Act of 1782. This is certainly true but, against this, we are entitled to urge that the entire drift of the narrative offers us a view of Jason which would make it very easy to accept that he would take the path of conformity in the matter of religion if it suited his pocket to do so. We are not *told* this in so many words, of course, but Thady's dis-owning of Jason might help to suggest it, and the ruthless Jason would be unlikely to be held back by a mere detail. In the light of all this, Flanagan's suggestion that 'some of the puzzles of the novel are resolved' if we take the view that the Rackrents have conformed acquires an added force. Mr Colgan's view of the matter, if correct, would certainly raise radical questions about Maria Edgeworth's deliberate ignoring of the facts of history. His essay, 'The Significant Silences of Thady Quirke', which is to be published in 1979, embodies the main arguments of his I.A.S.A.I.L. paper and should stimulate lively and fruitful discussion of the novel.

About certain areas of Thady's revelations there can be no doubt at all. His account of the Skinflint widow's rapacity, for example, clearly constitutes a powerful condemnation by the author of the practices there detailed:

> ... my lady was very charitable in her own way. She had a charity school for poor children, where they were taught to read and write gratis, and where they were kept well to spinning gratis for my lady in return; for she always had heaps of duty yarn from the tenants, and got all her household linen out of the estate from first to last; for after the spinning, the weavers on the estate took it in hand for nothing, because of the looms my lady's interest could get from the Linen Board to distribute gratis. Then there was a bleach yard near us, and the tenant dare refuse my lady nothing, for fear of a law-suit Sir Murtagh kept hanging over him about the water course. With these ways of managing, 'tis surprising how cheap my lady got things done, and how proud she was of it. Her table the same way— kept for next to nothing—duty fowls, and duty turkies, and duty geese, came as fast as we could eat 'em, for my lady kept a sharp look out, and knew to a tub of butter every thing the tenants had, all round. They knew her way, and what with fear of driving for rent and Sir Murtagh's law-suits, they were kept in such good order, they never thought of coming near Castle Stopgap without a present of something or other—nothing too much or too little for my lady—eggs—honey—butter—meal— fish—game, grouse, and herrings, fresh or salt—all went for something. As for their young pigs, we had them, and the best bacon and hams they could make up, with all young chickens in spring; but they were a set of poor wretches ... .

33

This entire passage is scathing in its ironies and ruthless in its exposure of the sheer cruelty involved in bleeding white an already oppressed tenantry. As the account continues and we learn that Sir Murtagh joined in the horrid game, making 'English tenants of them' and 'always driving and driving, and pounding and pounding, and canting and canting, and replevying and replevying' we feel almost that we are reading about the social lunacies of pre-revolutionary France and can hear the rumble of distant tumbrils. Marilyn Butler tells us that Richard Lovell Edgeworth, on arrival in Ireland in 1782, exactly reversed the pattern of Sir Murtagh's villainies:

> He abolished *duty work* and *duty fowl,* although the old leases still entitled him to these .... Furthermore, he recognized that the insecurity of land tenure in Ireland was one of the peasants' greatest hardships. He granted *de facto tenant right* to those who had improved their land or were visibly industrious.

There can be no doubt about Maria Edgworth's attitude to the Skinflint widow's 'charitable' doings and the oppressive behaviour of Sir Murtagh. Equally, the absentee Sir Kit who succeeds him is roundly condemned for his neglect of his tenants and for subjecting them to the vicious middleman who evicts them from their holdings so as to let them to other tenants at higher rents, to fuel Sir Kit's London extravagances.

Thomas Flanagan refers perceptively to 'the curiously enigmatic quality which is a source of the novel's power' and rightly relates this quality first of all to the author's use of Thady as her narrator, in a capacity which sets in motion an effective antithesis between Thady's story and Thady's understanding of that story. Independently of Thady, Maria Edgeworth also provides her Rackrents with a symbolically symmetrical pattern of doom. They marry badly, they sire no children, they lose out to their wives. Each has his absurd obsession: Patrick with ruinously lavish hospitality; Murtagh with litigation; Kit with money and duelling. Each of them dies madly. Furthermore, as Thady tells it, there is a kind of crazy comedy running through it all, which imparts to his narrative a *frisson* of particular horror.

One recalls, for example, the comic play made with Sir Kit's cruel vengence on his Jewish wife in having pig meat of all kinds brought to her table against her wishes, even though she has visited the cook in her kitchen for the precise purpose of averting this. One is moved to wonder whether the food with which he pesters her when she is imprisoned for seven years may not also be the hated sausages! Comically, when she is unexpectedly released by Sir Kit's death, her first act is to sack the cook. There is a sort of Chaucerian impishness here in the handling of detail, a distinctive glee in the midst of satire.

As she is careful to indicate in a note, Maria Edgeworth had not invented the story of the imprisoned wife but had based the incident on the actual imprisonment of Lady Cathcart by her husband for a very much longer period. The effective comic detail, however, is very much her own and this sardonic undertone is everywhere in the book, particularly in the first part, where the craziness of the Rackrents seems to rage most wildly. The novel has often been commended as a work of profound historical significance. What has scarcely ever been remarked is that it is also an amazingly funny book, riddled with a kind of demented laughter, which always works effectively to undercut pretension and to enlarge the novel's moral force. The swaggering Sir Kit, who throws a guinea to the servile Thady with such bravura, cuts a very different figure as he is brought home from his last duel 'up the avenue on the hand-barrow' while his wife watches incredulously from her window, scarcely able to believe that the tables have been so thoroughly turned on her bizarre spouse. The alcoholically hospitable Sir Patrick is granted the final Irish accolade, a fine funeral, but 'just as all was going on right, through his own town they were passing, when the body was seized for debt'. The litigious Sir Murtagh, so proud of his forensic capacities, is literally talked to death by his domestic opponent, the Skinflint widow, and bursts a blood-vessel while the servants crowd the back stairs to eavesdrop on his final apoplectic submissions. We are told by Maria's innocently sinister surrogate that 'all the law in the land could do nothing in that case'.

There is an unmistakeable darkening of the tone of the work in the second part, the 'History of Sir Conolly Rackrent'. Where the earlier Rackrents are tragi-comic zanies, Sir Condy is pitiable. Alone of them all, he is a figure for whom the reader can feel real affection. It is in this section of the work, also, that Jason Quirk begins to move to the centre of the stage. Sir Kit has earlier made the dangerous error of appointing Jason as his agent and we are now to see the full consequences of this. Sir Condy, last of the Rackrents, is in every way different from his predecessors. In particular, he is of lowlier origins. He has attended the local school and Thady can remember him 'bare-footed and bare-headed, running through the street of O'Shaughlin's town, and playing at pitch and toss, ball, marbles, and what not, with the boys of the town, amongst whom my son Jason was a great favourite with him'. The early relationships between Thady and Condy and between Condy and Jason are suggested with marvellous tact. 'He was ever my white-headed boy', Thady tells us, and goes on to recall how Condy as a child would sit on his knee to be told stories of 'the family and the blood from which he was sprung'. A splendidly deft touch is the casual information that, while Jason and Condy were at school together, the more able Jason had been 'not a little useful to him in his book-learning, which he acknowledged with gratitude ever after'. How cleverly this points the way to Jason's ruthless manipulation of Condy's affairs later! Poor Sir Condy never has a chance, coming into his property after he has borrowed heavily in advance against his expectations, and Jason moves swiftly to the attack:

> My son Jason, who was now established agent, and knew every thing, explained matters out of the face to Sir Conolly, and made him sensible of his embarrassed situation. With a great nominal rent-roll, it was almost

all paid away in interest, which being for convenience suffered to run on, soon doubled the principal, and Sir Condy was obligated to pass new bonds for the interest, now grown principal, and so on. Whilst this was going on, my son requiring to be paid for his trouble, and many years service in the family gratis, and Sir Condy not willing to take his affairs into his own hands, or to look them even in the face, he gave my son a bargain of some acres which fell out of lease at a reasonable rent; Jason set the land as soon as his lease was sealed to under-tenants, to make the rent, and got two hundred a year profit rent, which was little enough, considering his long agency.

Thady seems here to be attempting to justify Jason's behaviour, in a manner which reminds us of his earlier efforts on Jason's behalf during Sir Kit's residence in London, when Thady 'spoke a good word for my son and gave out in the country that nobody need bid against us', thereby assuring Jason of his first foot-hold on Rackrent land. Maria Edgeworth controls with consummate skill the balance between Thady's paternal commitment to Jason and his fidelity to Sir Condy. Perhaps the cleverest part of her contrivings has to do with the moment when Thady, flown with wine and his master's parliamentary triumph, betrays Sir Condy to the writ-server who, introduced to Jason by Thady himself, then conspires with Jason against Sir Condy. It is made very clear that Thady is quite drunk at this point:

> And of what passed after this I'm not sensible, for we drank Sir Condy's good health and the downfall of his enemies till we could stand no longer ourselves—and little did I think at that time, or till long after, how I was harbouring my poor master's greatest of enemies myself.

Nor does Thady know of Jason's collusion with this man until he sees his son's name coupled with the other's on the legal papers which are brought to bear on Sir Condy in connection with his debts:

> In the spring it was the villain that got the list of the debts from him brought down the custodiam, Sir Condy still attending his duty in Parliament; and I could scarcely believe my own eyes, or the spectacles with which I read it, when I was shown my son Jason's name joined in the custodiam; but he told me it was only for form's sake, and to make things easier, than if all the land was under the power of a total stranger.—Well, I did not know what to think—it was hard to be talking ill of my own, and I could not but grieve for my poor master's fine estate, all torn by these vultures of the law; so I said nothing, but just looked on to see how it would all end.

A close reading of the novel will find Thady neither ingenuous nor malign. What Maria Edgeworth has given us in this, her greatest achievement in the realm of characterisation, is a magnificently realised slave, a terrifying vision of the results of colonial misrule. There must have been a moment of clearly deliberate artistic decision in which she realised that what needed to be said must be said through one of the submerged people. Corkery and critics of his type may be justified in their own way when they lament the silence of the vast mass of the Irish people in the literature of the age but surely *Castle Rackrent* is the most powerful condemnation in existence of the forces of misrule which Corkery so thoroughly deplored? The remarkable combination of viewpoints which Maria Edgeworth achieved in Thady is a triumph beyond the reach of carping criticism. It is, in the circumstances of the time which produced it, a marvel of artistic vision and control. The novel's essential power derives from a relentless realism in the writer which enabled her to see present evils and their past causes, combined with a profound imaginative sympathy for the figure to whom she assigns the telling of the story. The South African poet, Roy Campbell, surveying a modern slave state, summed up similar tormenting contradictions in his tensely powerful sonnet, *The Serf:*

> His heart, more deeply than he wounds the plain,
> Long by the rasping share of insult torn,
> Red clod, to which the war-cry once was rain
> And tribal spears the fatal sheaves of corn,
> Lies fallow now. But as the turf divides
> I see in the slow progress of his strides
> Over the toppled clods and falling flowers,
> The timeless, surly, patience of the serf
> That moves the nearest to the naked earth
> And ploughs down palaces, and thrones, and towers.

Thady accompanies the ruined Sir Condy to the lodge, as the Fool accompanies Lear into the storm and, in so doing, rejects Jason and makes clear that rejection by concealing from his rapacious offspring the matter of the jointure which Sir Condy has settled on his wife, Isabella. The painful scene in which Jason finally confronts Sir Condy with the frightful reality of his total debt, while Thady hovers nearby, unable to understand anything except that his beloved master is being ruined by his own son, is as masterly in its way as the dark finale of Joseph Conrad's novel, *The Secret Agent,* where Winnie Verloc moves through madness and rage to a climax of horror. Maria Edgeworth never puts a foot wrong in this splendidly accumulated scene in which every detail is made to count, from the whiskey punch which Thady cannot bring himself to drink to the little children playing marbles in the street outside as Thady stumbles into the open, to get away from the unbearable sight of his master's undoing. Yet, there is no concession whatever to sentimentality at the end. Judy's part in the story is presented with cruel accuracy and she deservedly ends up with neither Condy nor Jason as husband. Her decline is conveyed with brutal candour by Thady:

> Poor Judy fell off greatly in her good looks after her being married a year
> or two, and being smoke-dried in the cabin and neglecting herself like, it
> was hard for Sir Condy himself to know her again till she spoke ... .

The finale of the novel shows us Thady doing, with characteristic fidelity, the office which his great-grandfather had long ago performed for the shaky Sir

Patrick, helping the doomed Sir Condy to fill the drink horn which will kill him. The ambivalence is consistent to the end.

Marilyn Butler suggests at one point in her biography that Maria Edgeworth 'did not in the least understand the nature of her own achievement as a novelist' and it may well be the case that, in this one book, the Edgeworthstown spinster was performing at a creative voltage more powerful than any she was later to generate, even in her other successful Irish novels. Butler quotes at length from a distressing and revealing letter which Maria wrote many years after *Rackrent,* in which the novelist recounted a harrowing incident involving a group of tenants on the Edgeworth estates. Three of the tenants voted in the election of 1835 for the White brothers, who were Liberals and Repealers. This meant they had opposed the Conservative candidate and voted against their landlord's interest. Sneyd Edgeworth, their legal landlord, was absent at the time but Barry Fox, husband of Sophy Edgeworth, decided to teach the recalcitrant tenants a harsh lesson by calling in their 'hanging-gale', a part of their rent which by custom had usually been left in arrear. Maria herself, as agent for the estate, was the one who had to receive payment of the money in question. The tenants involved were named Woods, Dermod and, significantly, Langan. The letter describing the incident is a long one and extraordinarily harrowing to read, as Maria depicts old Dermod trembling with conflicting emotions, so that he cannot count the money as he pays it over to her and Maria herself is filled with deep shame at the whole vile transaction:

> The thoughts of the number of years I had received rent from that good old tenant in my father's time all worked upon me. I am ashamed to tell you my finale—that tears began to flow, and though I twinkled and rubbed them out and off they did come—and Honora came in and Mr Hinds was by and it was all shameful.

The nearly seventy year old Maria who wept then at the shameful fiasco in which she found herself involved was the same Maria who many years earlier had penetrated in her best novel to an unforgettable imaginative sympathy with the conflicting loyalties of the sort of men who now stumbled and mumbled before her on this miserable day of the calling in of their hanging-gale. It is almost beyond belief that Marilyn Butler, elsewhere in her biography, can say of *Castle Rackrent* that 'if it exposes little, it also expresses little'. In fact, this biographer, for all her many excellences, seems generally unhappy in writing about this particular novel. She seems never to have resolved for herself the distinction between Maria the social theorist and Maria the writer of fiction. Butler sometimes writes about *Rackrent* as though Thady Quirk had wickedly taken over from his creator in a manner which the latter found unpalatable:

> It may be that Thady's dominance over the welter of incident gives the story more unity and perhaps more imaginative force than anything else Maria wrote, but it certainly does not allow the story to speak for her. She

found it unpalatable that she had made the quaint, archaic narrator more interesting than the Rackrents, who as landlords had in reality a more significant part to play in Irish life. Her motives in taking to fiction were not to act as an amanuensis to John Langan; on the contrary, the viewpoint she wanted to adopt was English and forward-looking. At the most personal level she had a good landlord in mind, and it had been impossible to get either him or his example into *Castle Rackrent.*

In the light of this, it is hardly surprising that Marilyn Butler is more at home with *The Absentee* and with *Ennui,* works which lack a dominant narrator and point a more conventional historical moral. *Pace* Marilyn Butler, however, *Castle Rackrent* remains Maria Edgeworth's most considerable work of fiction and continues to exert a powerful influence to the present day. At the centre of the work is the rotting house itself, that great symbolic focus of the Protestant Ascendancy's preoccupation with its own decline. The ruinous house haunted the dark imagination of Sheridan Le Fanu, it is everywhere in the novels of Lever, Somerville and Ross and George Moore. Most interesting of all, perhaps, is its re-appearance as a forceful symbol in modern Irish fiction, notably in the works of Jennifer Johnston, John Banville, J. G. Farrell and Aidan Higgins. Perhaps the recent Irish novel which approximates most closely to *Castle Rackrent* in conception and in the detail of its execution is Caroline Blackwood's black comedy, *Great Granny Webster.*

In 1834, in the letter to her half-brother cited earlier, Maria Edgeworth, while indicating that she could no longer attempt the depiction of Ireland in fiction, stated her intention of continuing to observe the Irish scene:

> Sir Walter Scott once said to me, 'Do explain to the public why Pat, who goes forward so well in other countries, is so miserable in his own'. A very difficult question: I fear above my power. But I shall think of it continually, and listen, and look, and read.

In one remarkable instance, at least, the matter of Ireland and the discerning analysis of its miseries was proved not to be 'above her power'. In *Castle Rackrent,* her listening, looking and reading had been bodied forth into one of the most incisive, profound and colourful creative fables in the whole of Anglo-Irish fiction.

Selected Bibliography

RELATED WORKS
Ennui, London, 1809.
Ormond, London, 1817 (Rpt Irish University Press, 1972).
Castle Rackrent is currently available in hbk from Dent in the Everyman series, and in pbk from Oxford U.P., ed. George Watson.

BIOGRAPHY
Emily Lawless, *Maria Edgeworth,* London, 1904.
Isabel C. Clarke, *Maria Edgeworth: Her Family and Friends,* London, 1950.
Elizabeth Inglis-Jones, *The Great Maria,* London, 1959.
Marilyn Butler, *Maria Edgeworth: A Literary Biography,* Oxford, 1972.

CRITICAL STUDIES
Percy Howard Newby, *Maria Edgeworth,* London, 1950.
Thomas Flanagan, *The Irish Novelists, 1800-1850,* New York, 1959, 53-106.
James Newcomer, *Maria Edgeworth the Novelist,* Forth Worth, 1967.
O. Elizabeth McWhorter Harden, *Maria Edgeworth's Art of Prose Fiction,* The Hague, Mouton, 1971.

CRITICAL ARTICLES
Roger McHugh, 'Maria Edgeworth's Irish Novels', *Studies,* xxvii (1938), 556-70.
George Watson, Preface to his edition of *Castle Rackrent,* Oxford English Novels series, 1964.
Patrick Murray, 'Maria Edgeworth and Her Father: The Literary Partnership', *Eire-Ireland* (Autumn 1971), 39-50.
Eileen Kennedy, 'Genesis of a Fiction: the Edgeworth-Turgenev relationship', *English Language Notes,* vi, 1969, 271-73.
Maurice Colgan, 'The Significant Silences of Thady Quirk', in *Social Roles for the Artist* (editors, Ann Thompson and Anthony Beck), University of Liverpool, 1979.

II

John Banim
THE NOWLANS

John Banim 1798~1842

John Banim was born in Kilkenny, the second son of a small farmer and shopkeeper, Michael Banim. He got his early education at various local schools and at the age of thirteen was sent to the celebrated Kilkenny College. Two years later he was sent to Dublin to attend classes at the Royal Dublin Society, with the intention of becoming an artist. He spent two years there and did well at his studies, winning a prize for his drawings during his first year. When he returned to his home town he began to work as an artist and a teacher of drawing. He fell passionately in love with one of his pupils, the natural daughter of a local gentleman, but was rejected as a suitor by her father. The girl was removed from Kilkenny to get her away from Banim and died shortly afterwards of tuberculosis. This early disappointment in love seems to have affected Banim grievously and his biographer, Patrick Joseph Murray, traces the illness which killed him eventually to his experiences at this early stage. He was to suffer constant ill-health throughout his life.

He began to contribute articles to the *Leinster Gazette* and set off again for Dublin in 1820 to embark on a career as a writer. He had no great success and thought of leaving for London but did not do so immediately. He published a long poem called *The Celt's Paradise* in 1823 and then turned to the writing of plays. His first effort in this form, *Turgesius,* was rejected by both Drury Lane and Covent Garden theatres but, in 1821, Macready accepted his next play, *Damon and Pythias,* and produced it at Covent Garden in May of that year, taking the part of Damon himself. This was Banim's first real literary success. He now began to plan, with his older brother Michael, their collaboration on the *Tales by the O'Hara Family.* They decided to use the pseudonyms of Abel O'Hara (John) and Barnes O'Hara (Michael) and agreed that they should act as critics of each other's work. Michael was reluctant to attempt creative writing but John detected in him a talent for forcefully realistic narrative and pressed him to make the attempt.

John married a Kilkenny girl, Ellen Ruth, in 1822 and soon after went to live in London where he worked as a journalist and as a librettist for the English Opera House whose proprietor, Thomas Arnold, became a friend of Banim and provided him with helpful commissions. Michael forwarded the story, *Crohoore of the Bill Hook,* to John in London in 1823 and John got busy on two stories, *John Doe* and *The Fetches.* The three tales were published in 1825 as the first series of the 'O'Hara' stories. They sold well and John now began work on his long, historical novel, *The Boyne Water,* travelling extensively in the north of Ireland to research his material. The book appeared in 1826 and later in the same year the second series of *Tales by the O'Hara Family* was also published. The second series was John's only and contained what many reckon to be his best work, *The Nowlans.* The other story in this series was a less important one, *Peter of the Castle.* Illness was already seriously affecting John by now and when Michael visited him in

London in 1826 he was shocked by his brother's appearance and reported that, although he was only twenty eight, he looked at least forty and was already manifesting clear signs of the dreadful illness which was soon to become chronic and eventually turn him into a permanent invalid, unable to walk without assistance and often assailed by savage attacks of severe muscular pain. In 1827 the third series of the 'O'Hara' tales was published, consisting of a novel by Michael, *The Croppy*.

In 1829 ill-health forced John to move to France in the hope that a change of climate might effect an improvement in his condition but a letter he wrote to Michael in May of the following year describes him as 'a paralysed man' and he was to find neither health nor fortune in France. In fact, he found himself in severe financial difficulties and, in 1832, his dreadful health was further weakened by an attack of cholera which almost killed him. His friends now came to his assistance and subscription lists on his behalf were opened in London, Dublin and Kilkenny. These benefactions enabled him to pay off some of his heavy debts but misfortune continued to dog him. His two small sons died, leaving him with only one child, a daughter. He decided to return to Ireland but was held up at Boulogne where his wife contracted typhus and they had to await her recovery before setting out for London. He arrived in Dublin in 1835 and managed to attend a benefit performance of two of his plays at the Theatre Royal. In September he reached Kilkenny where his brother was profoundly shocked by the appalling deterioration in his condition. John now settled down in a cottage to which he gave the name of 'Windgap Cottage'. Here he was visited by various friends and benefactors. Gerald Griffin, whom he had generously befriended in his London days, came to visit his old friend in 1836 and the two writers who had done so much to elevate the national dignity of their country by their fiction derived great joy from their reunion. In 1836, also, John Banim was granted a Civil List pension of £150, with an additional £40 for his young daughter. The story entitled *Fr Connell* was the last work on which he collaborated with his brother. John Banim died at Windgap Cottage in July of 1842. His brother Michael survived him by over thirty years and was to publish a number of works under his own name after John's early death. Michael died in 1874.

THE NOWLANS

In 1825, John Banim was at work on his elaborate novel, *The Boyne Water* and, to furnish himself with material for this ambitious imitation of Sir Walter Scott, he travelled extensively in the north of Ireland. Time, however, was short and he was forced to enlist the aid of his brother, Michael, for the researching of material which had to do with the southern region of the country. It was Michael who provided descriptions of Limerick and the surrounding area for the part of the novel which deals with Sarsfield and the siege and it was while he was touring the country for this purpose that Michael happened on the family who were to provide the basis for John's most powerful work of fiction. Michael recounts the incident in a lengthy letter to John's biographer, Patrick Murray. He describes how he travelled on foot through the Slieve Bloom mountains, making copious notes as he went, on the scenery and the people, sometimes being mistaken for a gauger on the look-out for illicit stills but managing to convince the local people of his real intentions:

> It was my fate to seek shelter for the night at the house of a farmer named Daniel Kennedy. His warm and comfortable dwelling was in a mountain hollow, known as Fail Dhuiv, or the Black Glen. The peculiarities of this out of the way homestead, the appearance of the dwellers therein, and the details of the unostentatiously hospitable reception given to me, were faithfully reported in my note-book. Extracted thence, almost word for word, my veritable account forms the introduction to the tale of 'The Nowlans'. There was a sick son on the night of my visit occupying the stranger's bedroom, about whom the good woman of the house and her daughters appeared to be most anxious.

Michael goes on to recount how, because the sick man was in occupation of the only guest-room in the cottage, he himself had to be accommodated with a bed made up on the kitchen table. In due course, all the details of this visit were pressed into service by John Banim, to form the introductory letter to *The Nowlans,* in which John, in his persona as 'Abel O'Hara' addresses a letter to 'Barnes O'Hara' in which Michael's account of his chance visit to the Kennedy house is made full use of and the story of 'priest John' is set in motion. *The Nowlans* formed Vols 1 and 2 of the second series of *Tales by the O'Hara Family,* published late in 1826. Vol. 3 contained the less important tale, *Peter of the Castle.* The customary debate on the matter of the brothers' collaboration can be dispensed with in this case, since, apart from the initial impetus provided by Michael, *The Nowlans* is John's work.

Mark Hawthorne has observed the special effectiveness of the epistolary opening of the tale:

> Because he introduced the characters in this chatty letter as if they were, indeed, actual men and women, the tale itself takes on an atmosphere of actuality. The family he met that wet August night had undergone its struggles: already "Father" John was in the cabin suffering from fever,

45

Peery Connolly was mad, and Peggy was being courted by Davy Shearman. In short, John began with the suggestions that the family had survived the trials that form the substance of the tale itself and that he was merely reporting what had happened. But the introductory letter does more. By relating the conclusion of the tale first, he removed much of the suspense so that his focus was on character; he concentrated on the development of his hero and heroine, carefully tracing the steps that led them to the opening pages of the letter.

This concentration on reality and on the analysis of character accords with views expressed by John Banim in his correspondence with Michael. John, ever the tutor in matters of literary technique, wrote regularly from London to his brother in Ireland, counselling him about the proper methods to be adopted in the writing of fiction. Murray quotes generously from such letters in his biography. John was the brother who had begun to make a name for himself as a professional writer and it was he who had first noticed Michael's genuine talent for the depiction of Irish rural character and incident and had urged his brother to persevere and to collaborate with him on various tales. John's advice was dispensed in the most acceptable manner, as the brothers regularly exchanged their work and vigorous criticism was a two-way process, with John urging Michael to criticise his own work as severely as he can and to call upon the whole family to join in the work of judgement. In a long letter of May 24, 1824, John writes:

> I send you the MSS. of my tale, and I request your severest criticisms; scratch, cut, and condemn at your pleasure. This is the first copy. Looking over it, I perceive many parts that are bad; send it back when you can, with every suggestion you are capable of making. Read it for the whole family in solemn conclave. Let father, mother, Joanna and yourself sit in judgement on it, and send me all your opinions sincerely given.

Advice from someone who was so willing to submit his own work to vigorous criticism must have proved easy to accept. In this same letter, John notes that two of the characters in one of Michael's tales 'do not stand out sufficiently from the canvas' and urges him to 'aim at distinctness and individuality of character'. He goes on to remind Michael of some of the amusing characters they have both known in their native Kilkenny, pointing up their individual peculiarities and identifying those traits which make them memorable. The entire drift of his advice to Michael has to do with the vivid and dynamic depiction of real people who will impress the reader with their individual appearances, their distinctive attitudes of mind and their particular modes of speech. The novelist must aim at dramatising his tale in a manner faithful to life itself. 'Plot', John significantly concludes, 'is an inferior consideration to drama, though still it is a main consideration'. His preference for vividly dramatic characters is reminiscent of his friend Gerald Griffin's fondness for strong scenes which could be acted out by the great stage figures of the day such as Macready and Kean. Both Banim and Griffin had tried their hands at stage plays, without much success, and their interest in strong fictional realism gave their prose works, both novels and short stories, a colourful richness of texture. Faithful to his own prescription, John Banim was to achieve in *The Nowlans* a work which, in the realms of character analysis and the exploration of motives, often approaches greatness but one which is also, in places, quite execrably plotted.

Broadly speaking, the work falls into three main sections, the first two dealing with 'priest' John's relationships with Maggy Nowlan and with Letty Adams. The third, by far the most confused and chaotic, recounts the fortunes of John's sister, Peggy Nowlan, and her relationship with the villain of the piece, Letty's brother, Frank Adams. As Hawthorne remarks, 'the first volume develops a psychological dilemma; the second shows people in fanatic, superficial action'. Banim grounds his work firmly in precisely the manner which he had recommended to his brother, offering us an entirely convincing picture of John Nowlan's parents and their setting. His father, Daniel Nowlan, is a small farmer who has prospered through the high prices paid for farm produce during the Napoleonic wars. Daniel, to the surprise of his neighbours, chooses as his bride a "black protestant", one, moreover, 'allied, as she had pride in boasting, to one of the least popular protestant families in Tipperary, of which the head was a county magistrate, and two of the younger sons chiefs of police'.

In assigning John Nowlan one Catholic and one Protestant parent, Banim both provides himself with a splendid opportunity for entertaining characterisation and also furnishes his work with an appropriate sectarian ambivalence which is relevant to the entire social fabric of the work and to the hero's main dilemma. Throughout, the novel will seek to explore the divided Ireland of the early nineteenth century, an Ireland which saw the proselytising activities of the 'New Reformation' in full swing, an Ireland where all that was solid and respectable was also Protestant, where the vast majority of the people were Catholics struggling desperately to achieve some sort of civic identity for the first time since the inception of the Penal Laws. Throughout the work also, John Nowlan will be subjected to moral and social pressures from the two sides of the religious divide and will be made to question the absolutes of clerical celibacy and the rigid regulations of the Church in which he has taken his vows as a clergyman. The immensely diverting account which Banim provides of Mrs Nowlan's partial 'conversion' from her original Protestantism to her husband's faith, forms an ironically comic prelude to the genuine agonies of indecision which will afflict her son later in the work. Not until Joyce offers us his portrait of that most reluctant of Catholics, Mr Kernan of the short story, *Grace,* will we encounter so amusing a study of divided religious allegiances as Mrs Nowlan:

> She had been brought up decidedly biased to one religion, chiefly because
> hating the other; and not much burdened, even after her conversion, with
> a knowledge of the distinctions between both, Mrs Nowlan was,

sometimes, indifferently and unconsciously a child of either. For instance; while giving out, during Lent, at the head of her domestics and children, the form of prayer called "the rosary", ... Mrs Nowlan more than once mixed up, in a concluding aspiration, the first of a Roman Catholic prayer and the last of a Protestant one ... .

Sometimes, Mrs Nowlan will set out to attend Mass and will arrive instead at the local Protestant church. At other times, she will go to Mass with her husband but will sit and read the Book of Common Prayer throughout the service. In discussions at her own fireside, she will sometimes quite forget that she is now officially a Catholic and will launch into spirited attacks on the practices of her adopted Church. She is at all times proud of her connection with her well-to-do Protestant relatives and has a tendency to list them in her evening prayers when called upon to pray for the 'repose of the souls of the faithful departed'. As presented by Banim, Mrs Nowlan becomes a comically idiosyncratic character of a highly effective kind, in the manner which John Banim had recommended to his brother, but there is a cutting edge to this comedy, since Mrs Nowlan's absurd social pretensions reflect the social pretensions of Irish Protestants in general and expose the ruinous divisions in the society with which the novel is profoundly concerned:

> While to catholicism she owed all the pride of being a married woman, a mother, and an independent person, protestantism conferred upon her other honours not to be forgotten, such as the pride of civil rank and superior caste; for many obscure, vulgar-named, and vulgarly descended protestant families, in Ireland, (who, in England, or Scotland, could not find an ancestor, or one of their own name elevated out of the lower classes of honest handicraft or tradesfolk) used to consider themselves, merely as protestants, a race of beings as much above Irish papists, as white men above black ... .

Unhappily for young John Nowlan, the man who is to have the most powerful influence on his early development is a wealthy but stupid Catholic who dissipates a vast fortune in aping his Protestant 'betters'. This is his father's brother, Aby Nowlan, the eldest of four sons and the sole heir to an estate of a thousand a year from many farms accumulated by his thrifty father. Aby, the first Catholic 'gentleman farmer' of the district is a licentious dolt who acquires many mistresses and a string of bastards and fills his house with drunken local squireens and hangers-on who gradually devour his substance. Mrs Nowlan hopes that Aby will adopt young John as his special protegé. Aby is John's god-father and is thought to have a soft spot for the boy and it is on this skimpy assumption that all his mother's foolish hopes are built. Whenever Aby rides by the Nowlans' house and bids the family the time of day, young John is handed up to him to be kissed and fondled by his wealthy uncle and Mrs Nowlan continues to cherish her silly hopes for John's adoption by the oafish but wealthy Aby. Aby does nothing much to encourage her hopes but neither does he in any way contradict them and, after a long time during which Mrs Nowlan has almost resigned herself to abandoning her dreams, John comes to his uncle's favourable notice by standing up for him in public when Aby and his latest mistress are being condemned by the local priest from the altar during Mass. In gratitude, Aby takes young John to live with him in his appallingly rackety household and it is thus that John is launched on the career of lurid sensuality which is to be his downfall. John has already begun to study for the priesthood, a course on which his mother decided to launch him when his uncle Aby appeared to have lost interest in the boy. Thus, the vocation of the priesthood has been hit on by the family as second-best to the possibility of adoption by his uncle Aby and the boy is set to learning Latin so that he may in due course go to 'the Bishop's school' at Limerick and study for the Church. His dangerously pragmatic mother spells out the realities of Irish rural life as she sees them, as she despatches her seventeen-year old boy to live in what she well knows to be a cross between a disorderly ale-house and a brothel:

> ... a priest's a good thing, Johnny, more betoken at the end of a score of years, or so, whin he's snug in the glebe-house—the parish-priest's house, I mane; bud a gintleman is a good thing, too, at the head o' the thousands iv acres, an' if he likes to live a life as good as a priest, an' not curse or swear, or dhrink, or do other things, like some one we know, an' goes to his duty every sacrament Sunday, why, thin, Johnny, he's as good as the priest in one regard, an' betther in another ... .

She accompanies this grossly worldly counsel with a hypocritical prayer, 'God for ever keep my oun good bouchal from harum', a prayer which, as the author is quick to inform us, the deity ignores.

John's sojourn in his Uncle Aby's dreadful house is vividly recounted. Little by little, against his natural inclinations, he finds himself drawn into the drunken carousing and the generally profligate ways of the disorderly camp-followers who regularly gather to scavenge on the stupid Aby. His uncle has chosen to model himself on his better-born, Protestant counterpart, Squire Adams of Mount Nelson, and to this end he keeps constant open house for the Squire's many sons and their equally greedy cronies. For the entertainment of these graceless and ungrateful parasites, food and drink of the most lavish kind is constantly being purchased from the local shopkeepers at high prices. At the same time, the current 'Mrs Aby' is engaged in entertaining a string of her own female cronies upstairs. John Nowlan soon comes to see that his uncle Aby is being rapidly brought close to ruin by all this unnecessary expense but he cannot prevail on his foolish uncle to take any practical steps to cope with the creditors who now begin to press on him more and more. Furthermore, John soon realises that the promise made by his uncle that he will be sent to a good school in Limerick will not be kept and he tries to settle down to study in the uncongenial establishment of which he now finds himself part:

> John, despairing, in time, of being sent to school, and sick of the miserable scene around him, arranged in a little bed-room, which he had with much difficulty got his uncle to appoint exclusively for him, his

humble set of books, English and Latin; namely, a Murray's and a Lilly's Grammar; the History of Ireland, in one volume, written by a silly schoolmaster; Goldsmith's paltry History of England; a small Geography; a few odd volumes of the Spectator; "Scott's Lessons", a school reading-book of Pieces in prose and verse ... in this chamber he strove to detach his mind from the disagreeable and sometimes bad impressions it was receiving; but with little effect.

John's severest temptation comes from one of his Uncle Aby's by-blows, his young cousin Maggy Nowlan, whom he first encounters when she is a wayward child of twelve. At first, he undertakes to tutor her but she proves a careless and indifferent pupil and soon sets about her main business of seducing 'priest John'. She turns her reading lessons into little love sessions, kissing and caressing her handsome young cousin in a pretence of cousinly affection, well knowing that she is fanning his emerging sexuality to a flame of desire. The tormented John does his best to avoid his temptress. He shuts himself up in his room to study and pray, but Maggy will not leave him in peace. She passes by his door, leaves messages for him in his room and he is never allowed to forget her alluring nearness. Banim depicts the fluctuations of his passion and his fits of repentance with great skill, effectively relating the gradual coarsening of his nature to the vile atmosphere of his uncle's house and the evil courses in which his continued residence there inevitably involves him:

> This was the time that he became more than ever engaged in riding about to the tenants, in endeavouring to pacify creditors, and in stratagems for his uncle's existence and personal safety. And such a course of life tended, in a way different from his feelings for Maggy, to sully his boyish purity of character, and give that mixed one, which leaves its possessor open to grave danger for the remainder of his existence. Wrangling with the mean tenants made him, in some degree, mean also—at least he *felt* it did; putting off the creditors taught him to speak things that were not true; the necessity of countenancing the sheriff's sons, and even the lower law officers, further involved that necessity of drinking more, and oftener, than he had ever done before ... .

Thus, gradually, he falls away from his earlier ideals and his character deteriorates as his uncle's fortunes decline. Maggy's mother, Mrs Carey, now brazenly offers her daughter to John, pointing out that Aby 'intends to give her a purty penny' and offering the pair her dubious blessing. Maggy comes to his room one night and tries quite brazenly to seduce him but he thrusts her away from him, realising that she and her mother are trying to bring about his downfall. The atmosphere of tense and sleazy passion evoked by Banim in this part of his story is as ugly and authentic as that which Hardy builds around Jude Fawley and Arabella Donn but Banim does not permit Maggy to bring her attempt at seduction to a successful climax. The insulting words with which 'priest John' rejects her will continue to rankle and will help to turn her into a vicious and dangerous foe. Aby's profligacy and foolishness finally bring the bailiffs upon him and he is forced to take refuge in his brother Daniel's house. Thus, instead of John's fortune being made by his wealthy uncle Aby, a ruined Aby is forced to spend his last days as a beggar under John's father's roof. All Mrs Nowlan's grandiose plans for John are in ruins. Aby finally suffers a stroke while sitting at the fireside with the appalled John who is horrified by the sudden manner of his uncle's unheralded death:

> John Nowlan felt shocked and troubled at the bottom of his soul, upon
> the death of his uncle. The convulsed face, the staring, glassy eyes, the
> distorted limb, haunted his thoughts, day and night,for months. He slept
> little; and nothing else found place in his reflections. Maggy was forgotten.
> No fiery passions could riot in the awed stupor of soul he now
> experienced.

Abandoned by John, Maggy falls in with a stranger and bears him a child. She refuses to name her seducer and tries to involve herself with John Nowlan once again, coming to him to solicit his help for herself, her mother and her child. As he is about to submit to her blandishments, John is rescued in the nick of time by his old friend, the parish priest who has come to conduct a 'station' in the Nowlans' house. In a characteristic plunge from temptation to virtue, John Nowlan now goes to live at the priest's house and embarks once again on his studies for the priesthood. Yet, the very completeness and abruptness of his reversion to a saintly and scholarly mode of life has warned us that his passionate nature will place him at risk again. Banim is charting here, with great boldness and frankness and considerable psychological insight, violent impulses like those which affect James Joyce's Stephen Dedalus. Like Dedalus, John Nowlan embarks on a careful regimen of orderly living and pious practices but his original innocence has been spoilt forever and his next temptation will assume a subtler and more effective form.

It comes to him four years later as the result of a chance meeting with Letty Adams, one of Squire Adams' many daughters. She, with her brother, Frank, and her uncle, Mr Long, takes refuge in the Nowlans' cottage from a sudden storm and this accidental encounter not only brings together John and Letty Adams but also throws Peggy Nowlan in the way of Frank Adams, who appears first in the story merely as the student brother of Letty but will, as the tale advances, regrettably become the increasingly Gothic villain of the novel. John Nowlan has already been subjected to the comparatively straightforward pressures of mere sexual desire, during his early relationship with Maggy Nowlan. Banim acutely distinguishes between those gross youthful impulses and the feelings which John now begins to entertain for the very different Letty Adams, showing how the manifest differences between the two women delude John into a serious misunderstanding of the threat which Letty Adams poses to his peace of mind and to his clerical vocation:

> His feelings for poor Maggy Nowlan were distinct; from their
> distinctness, alarming; and therefore he might, if he liked have struggled
> against them; even while coming on, they gave their rattle-snake warning:

but the different kind of passion that now stole to his heart was unobservable, silent, insidious; a beautiful snake winding through fields of flowers to sting him as he lay asleep. Because his blood did not flame in the presence of the new syren, as it used to do by the side of his unhappy cousin, he never thought himself in danger. The very purity of the love he began for the first time to feel, left him unguarded against its possible vehemence.

He lusted after Maggy and thought it love. Those earlier desires bear no relationship to his newly awakening feelings for the beautiful and gentle Letty Adams so, to begin with, the newly reformed clerical student fails utterly to discern his new danger. Maggy was his uncle Aby's illegitimate daughter and, therefore, John's first cousin. She was an unlettered and amoral child of nature who flaunted herself before him and did her best to bed him. Letty is a young lady of good family, or, at the very least, of prosperous Protestant stock. She is refined and well schooled, elegantly attired and a charming conversationalist:

> When her manner, looks, and words conveyed, in spite of her, the first intimations of a growing love for him, he therefore rejoiced instead of trembling at symptoms that only seemed to bespeak what was, he thought, the liveliest ambition of his soul; a friendship and interest, harmless though strong and decided, on the part of a being whose good wishes were the highest honour he or any other person could receive.

Frank Adams begins to show an interest in Peggy Nowlan and the four young people are thrown together when Mr Long invites John and Peggy Nowlan to be his guests at his home. John begins to suspect that Frank Adams has designs on Peggy and also begins to assume that Peggy is falling in love with Frank. In fact, Peggy has sensibly seen through Frank from their very first encounter and has marked him down as a condescending Protestant upstart who treats her beloved brother John with a barely concealed contempt which infuriates her. She has noticed how Frank, recently returned from Oxford, despises John's schooling and his knowledge of the Classics. Ironically, of course, Frank has failed to distinguish himself in any way at the university and has, in fact, got into serious trouble there in connection with gambling but he feels free nevertheless to despise John Nowlan's rustic ways and the unsophisticated nature of his tastes. He dubs John 'clownish', signifying his ascendancy contempt for the young clerical student who has not enjoyed his own social and educational advantages. To begin with, however, he succeeds in concealing these views from John himself and the two young men appear to get on quite well together for a time. John hugely enjoys his stay at Mr Long's elegant house, relishing the excellent library it contains and delighting in the company of the beautiful Letty. Ominously, he undertakes to tutor her in Latin, as he had once undertaken to teach poor Maggy Nowlan to read, and when Peggy returns to her father's home, John stays on at Mr Long's house, meeting Letty daily and falling ever more deeply in love.

The Nowlans

Maggy Nowlan now re-enters the story, to tell John that she has become a Dublin prostitute and also to deceive him into suspecting that Frank and Peggy are lovers. The tempestuous John promptly tackles Frank about this but the latter manages to reassure him that his intentions in regard to Peggy are honourable ones and that he intends to marry her when he can do so without upsetting his Protestant relatives, particularly Mr Long, from whom he has expectations. Frank also taxes John with his own obvious interest in Letty but John insists that his clerical vows stand in the way of any such marital involvement and that his obivious regard for Letty is that of a friend, not of a lover. Frank Adams now proposes to John that he should seriously consider abandoning his Catholicism and instead become a Protestant clergyman, free to marry, a suggestion which shocks John and throws his mind into confusion. Frank furthers his own nefarious schemes by suggesting to his sister that John Nowlan has not taken his final vows as a priest and is, therefore, free to marry her. Letty, enamoured of John, is only too eager to believe her brother's lies and the unhappy couple become more involved with each other and tormented by the contradictions of their situation. Banim climaxes his first volume with an elaborate scene at the house of Squire Adams at Mount Nelson. John Nowlan is a troubled and watchful guest at the dinner-table where a motley group of proselytising clergymen is assembled. The notion implanted in his mind by Frank of abandoning his religion and going over to the fashionable creed of the ascendancy squireens, the creed to which place and privilege automatically attach themselves, has continued to torment him and he is now confronted by a former college friend of his, one Horrogan, who has already apostasised and is being employed by the Protestant missionary group to preach to the Irish poor in their native language, through which it is hoped they can be more easily persuaded to abandon their faith. Horrogan proves to be an uncouth simpleton of no great importance but the senior one among the Protestant missionaries, an Englishman named Stokes, is more sympathetically depicted by Banim though his complete incomprehension of the Irish and their religious affiliations is never in any doubt:

> Mr Sirr, a well-favoured and interesting young man, entered the parlour, introducing the Rev. Mr Stokes, an English clergyman, sent from a Bible Society in London to investigate the progress of their benevolent efforts among the peasantry of Ireland. The missionary, exercising to its utmost the self-pleased and urbane smile that never quite deserted his handsome old features, bowed round from his hips, in a way that said, "Yes, here I am, the agent of a body of good men, associated to do your poor benighted country a service above praise; here I stand among you, simple as a child, just as if I was no such important and graced individual: here I am, looking unconscious, as you see, of my superiority as an Englishman, an admired preacher, a philanthropist, and a perfected Christian".

This unctuous, well-meaning and rather silly figure is finally given his congé by an old Dominican friar, Mr Shanaghan, who has been presented with a

Bible earlier by the Protestant missionaries. Shanaghan is used by Banim to open Stokes' eyes to the real facts of the Catholic religion and to the thoughtless insult which has been dealt the friar by the missionaries' stupid assumption that he is ignorant of the scriptures. He is also made to comment cuttingly on the unprepossessing convert, Mr Horrogan. The entire scene at Squire Adams' noisy dinner-table is meant to convey to English readers something of the fabric of Irish life and to educate them about Irish Catholicism. It is, inevitably, a prosy affair, with a good deal of Irish history being fed into the exchanges. The principal interest of the scene in relation to the novel's more important concerns lies in John Nowlan's fascinated interest in the awful Horrogan, who has gone over to Protestantism, turning his back on his earlier Catholic clerical training. John is eager to have speech with Horrogan, to quiz him about his radical shift of religious allegiance. If Horrogan can change his coat in this way, perhaps John Nowlan may do likewise and thus entitle himself to Letty as the wife of his choice:

> ... John Nowlan regarded this specimen of a conversion with mixed alarm and interest. He felt it add another twitch to his impatience of the restraint which now held mortal combat with his constitutional throbbings after happiness. Letty before him, Frank at his elbow ... John trembled to find himself thinking—"as Horrogan has done, surely I may do:"—and he thrilled with anxiety to meet Horrogan alone, and call on him for a full statement of the convictions that had caused a change in his religious principles.

There is no escape for John by this route, however. When he manages to speak privately to Horrogan to enquire the reasons for his conversion, he finds his old schoolfellow to be a foolish sot who can produce no reasonable explanation of the course he has adopted, such as might justify John Nowlan in imitating him. The volume closes with his significant realisation that his own clerical vow 'may be broken, not forsworn'. He understands clearly now that, if he marries Letty, he must do so against the strict rules of his own Church and that he cannot escape his moral responsibilities by switching creeds.

This first volume of *The Nowlans* has shown John Banim writing often with great power and penetration on social issues and personal dilemmas which profoundly interested him. He was tackling what was, for his period, explosive material. His avowed purpose in all his fiction was to reveal his people in a true light to the readers of the larger island and it was extremely courageous of him to choose an errant priest as his hero for a full-length novel. He must have known the risks he ran of offending his fellow-countrymen by his choice of theme. In this respect, Banim is something of a pioneer and deserves high praise for his forthright approach to a sensitive subject. Irish fiction has produced plenty of sentimentalised portraits of priests of the 'soggarth aroon' kind but surprisingly few realistic portraits of priests as fallible, human figures subject to the stresses which beset all mortals.

John Nowlan is a worthy predecessor of George Moore's Fr Gogarty or Gerald O'Donovan's Fr Ralph. Only a few talented writers such as Richard Power or Brian Moore have offered us equally credible portraits of priests in contemporary fiction. It would, therefore, be very gratifying if one could maintain that Banim sustained this level of performance in the second volume of his story. Unfortunately, he did not. The second volume deals largely with Peggy Nowlan and Frank Adams and lapses into melodramatic contrivances of all kinds. The first of these has John Nowlan forcing Frank and Peggy into marriage because he has been deceived by Maggie Nowlan into the belief that Frank has seduced his sister. When this absurd match has been improbably celebrated by the friar, Shanaghan, John next rushes off to Dublin with Letty, committing himself totally to a course which he has failed utterly to justify to himself in terms of the morality by which he has lived as a clerical student and a priest.

John Nowlan's life with Letty in Dublin is depicted by Banim with a kind of morbid realism which is immensely powerful in conveying the mental torment he suffers and the physical privations they both undergo through poverty and loneliness. The hideously unpleasant lodgings in Phibsborough are brought to sordid life through the sort of detail which must surely owe something to Banim's own unhappy experiences in Dublin as a young man. The dreadful Mr and Mrs Grimes, the stingy owners of this mean household, are memorable portraits of a particular kind of smug parsimony. Oddly enough, Thomas Flanagan appears to feel that Banim had lost his objectivity in his depiction of the Grimes couple and their setting. He writes of Banim's imagination being 'liberated from its everlasting fairmindedness'. He appears to take the view that Banim is satirising a particular kind of Protestantism in his account of the Grimes pair and their unlovely residence. This seems to me to do less than justice to the effectiveness of the entire episode. John and Letty are allowed no idyllic interlude in their loving. He is convinced that, as a priest, he is not married at all and that he has, therefore, dragged Letty with him into the most fearsome kind of sinfulness. Letty, convinced by Frank that John has not taken final vows, appears to believe in the marriage as a real one, but they are, in any case, allowed little opportunity for speculation about the rights and wrongs of their union. The mere business of keeping body and soul together occupies them to the exclusion of all else. John, to begin with, manages to get some work as a teacher but his secret becomes known to the well-to-do Dublin Catholics who employ him and they soon reject him brutally, making it quite clear that they see him as a priest who is living in sin with a mistress. Thus, *pace* Flanagan, Banim seems to present just as unsympathetic a view of his Dublin Catholics as he does of the Protestant Grimes family. The former are as viciously uncharitable as the latter are meanly self-satisfied. John and Letty are rejected by all and their letters home provide no solution to their problems. Letty's letters to her uncle remain unanswered and she will die without knowing that Frank has thwarted her efforts to get in touch with her uncle. Eventually, poverty forces the unhappy pair to flee from Dublin and, soon after, Letty dies with her first-born in the direst poverty and John Nowlan lays out her body on an old door in a dreadful hovel by the roadside. This scene, which sounds like the worst kind of melodrama when recounted out of context, has in its place in the story a dark and gloomy power, providing a fitting climax to John Nowlan's doomed and hopeless passion.

The rest of the work lapses into the worst kind of lurid and improbable contrivance to the point where the reader can scarcely summon up the necessary energy or curiosity to follow the labyrinthine improbabilities of an increasingly silly plot. Frank Adams turns into the most Gothic of villains. There are attacks on stage coaches, disguises, fortunate rescues at the last minute, dark murders in ruined wayside cottages, nothing seems to be too highly-coloured or unconvincing to find its way into the story which meanders from Tipperary to Dublin and back again. John Nowlan, who has been at the centre of the tale from the beginning, disappears from view and Banim never succeeds in achieving the same penetration of the character of Peggy Nowlan. The powerful realism of the first volume gives way to lurid melodrama. The realities of Irish life are once again forced into the unsuitable form of nineteenth century sensational fiction. Mark Hawthorne, who has written perceptively on the mingling of English and Irish religious values in *The Nowlans,* also discerns at work in the book important symbolic patterns of light and darkness which he traces in considerable detail. Concerning the uneasy combination of realism and melodrama he has this to say:

> ... nowhere before had characters as Gothic as Frank, as evil as Maggy and her mother, or as innocent as Peggy joined a sensitive and intense portrayal of a young man's struggle between flesh and faith. By overly manipulating the plot in the second volume, Banim marred an otherwise fine novel, yet this manipulation is indicative of his difficulty in uniting English taste and Irish values. The characters he wanted to draw cannot fit into the formulae of the popular English novel, but he was reluctant to discard completely the plot that had reached maturity during the century before he wrote.

Sadly, Banim was prepared to tamper with what most readers feel is the strongest part of his work, his frank presentation of John Nowlan's powerful passions and his realistic depiction of the disorderly life of the lecherous Aby Nowlan. In a letter to his brother, Michael, on Christmas Day, 1826, John writes:

> The second series go on right well; but the publishers say they are too strongly written, too harrowing, and, in parts, too warm and impure. The latter portion of this judgement, I regret to say, is merited. I have made a mistake, and must not again fall into the same error.

In the following April, another letter to Michael indicates that the bowdlerising of *The Nowlans* has taken place:

The Nowlans

> In the second edition of the second series of our tales, just out, I have
> corrected some of the more glaring improprieties of the first.

His biographer, Murray, appears to approve of the alterations. Fortunately for Banim, his moralistic unease does not appear to have developed into the sort of general creative nausea which was to assail his friend, Gerald Griffin, and lead to that writer's complete abandonment of his craft. In thus altering the first version of his most powerful novel, Banim was merely adapting himself to the prudish moral standards of his day. Modern readers will return to the story's original and more powerful version and delight in its bold tackling of a soul-struggle of a turbulent and deeply disturbing nature.

In *The Nowlans,* John Banim, in spite of obtrusive and outmoded conventions, managed to chart the lonely and agonising moral struggle of a tormented and devious nature. He dealt with sexual matters with frankness and clarity and charted the shifts and vacillations of his hero in a manner convincingly geared to the action of the story. In his bold use of chance and coincidence and near-miss situations he anticipates the quality of the rustic tragedies of Thomas Hardy and his handling of John Nowlan's dark and lonely struggle against his own passionate nature is as modern as John McGahern's *The Dark.* Small wonder that Maria Edgeworth referred admiringly to *The Nowlans* as 'a work of great genius'. Yeats also thought highly of the first half of *The Nowlans.* He described it as 'terrible and frank' and identified in John Banim 'an abiding cold and dry-eyed sadness' which, Yeats felt, differentiated him from the more humorous Carleton. Yeats also remarked in Banim the mixture of realism and melodrama which is so noticeable in *The Nowlans:*

> John Banim and his brother Michael, who both have the true peasant
> accent, are much more unequal writers than Carleton. Unlike him, they
> covered the peasant life they knew with a melodramatic horde of pirates
> and wealthy libertines whom they did not know.

Yet, in spite of his largely unsuccessful struggle with the novel form, in spite, also, of appalling ill-health and a grievously arduous life, John Banim managed, in *The Nowlans,* to do enough to convince us of his considerable gifts as a novelist, combining a searching analysis of individual torment with a comprehensive dramatisation of the frustrating and contradictory Ireland of his day.

Selected Bibliography

RELATED·WORKS

Tales by the O'Hara Family, 1st Series, London, 1825.
The Boyne Water, London, 1826.
(pbk reprint, CERIUL, Université de Lille III, 1976).
The Smuggler, London, 1831.

BIOGRAPHY

Patrick Joseph Murray, *The Life of John Banim,* London, 1857.

CRITICAL STUDIES·

Thomas Flanagan, *The Irish Novelists 1800-1850,* New York, 1959, 167-202.
Mark D. Hawthorne, *John and Michael Banim (The "O'Hara Brothers"): A Study in the Early Development of the Anglo-Irish Novel,* Salzburg, 1975.

CRITICAL ARTICLES

Louis Lachal, 'Two Forgotten Irish Novelists', The Irish Monthly, Vol. 58 (1930), 338-49.
B. G. MacCarthy, 'Irish Regional Novelists of the Early Nineteenth Century', *The Dublin Magazine,* N.S., XXI, 3 (July-Sept. 1946), 28-37.

III

Gerald Griffin
THE COLLEGIANS

Gerald Griffin 1803-1840

Gerald Griffin was born in Limerick in 1803, the youngest surviving son of Patrick Joseph Griffin and Ellen Griffin, formerly Ellen Geary. The family was a well-connected, middle-class one. One of Ellen's brothers, John Geary, M.D., was the leading Limerick physician of his day and another of her brothers was the proprietor of a Limerick newspaper. Two of her sons, William and Daniel Griffin, were to become prosperous and distinguished doctors in their turn and eventually play a prominent part in the civic life of Limerick. Patrick, the novelist's father, tried his hand in turn at both farming and brewing but does not seem to have made a great success of either. In 1810, when Gerald was only seven years old, the family moved from Limerick to a house named 'Fairy Lawn', beautifully situated on a hill above the Shannon estuary about twenty eight miles from the city and it was here that Gerald spent the next ten formative years, growing up in beautiful surroundings which left a lasting mark on his poetic imagination. He was given a somewhat scrappy education, tutored at home by a visiting teacher to begin with and later attending a school at Limerick. Eventually, he was moved from his Limerick school and sent to a local school near 'Fairy Lawn' which was run by a rather unorthodox teacher named O'Donovan. This man seems to have been close to the hedge-school tradition and Gerald's eventual biographer, his brother Daniel, suggests that some of the comic scenes in Griffin's novels derive from his experiences in O'Donovan's school at this time.

In 1820 both Griffin parents and a large section of the family emigrated to Pennsylvania, leaving Gerald behind under the guardianship of his older brother, Dr William Griffin. Daniel and several of the sisters also remained in Ireland and went to live with William in Adare. This break-up of the loving, closely-knit family circle in which he had grown to young manhood was a cruel blow to Gerald. He never saw his parents again but continued to correspond with them and is said to have sent them the considerable sum of money, about £800, which he earned with his novel, *The Collegians,* nearly a decade after his parents' departure for America. When the time came for Gerald to decide on a career, he first thought of following William and Daniel into the medical profession but soon gave up this idea and decided instead to try to make his way as a writer. He met John Banim, the young Kilkenny writer, who had achieved some notice in 1821 when his play, *Damon and Pythias,* was given a London production by two leading actors of the day, Macready and Kemble. Gerald now wrote a play under the title of *Aguire,* showed it to his brother and sought his permission to go to London in order to try to make a career there as a playwright. William was favourably impressed by his young ward's first literary efforts but hesitant to permit the adventure at first. He gave way, however, and Gerald left for London late in 1823, in his nineteenth year.

In London, at first, he met with nothing but disappointment. Macready, to whom he submitted *Aguire,* eventually rejected the play without comment and Griffin spent the first six months of 1824 in despondency and poverty. He hid himself away in what he called a 'mouse-hole' of a lodging near St Paul's, refused to see even John Banim when his fellow-Irishman tried to come to his aid, and began to despair of ever making his way in London. He soon saw that the theatrical taste of the day was for gaudy and elaborate scenic effects and that the theatres were controlled by egocentric actor-managers intent only on their own careers. There was no place in such a theatrical world for the solemnly moral tragedies which Griffin wanted to present. Gradually, he began to abandon his dramatic ambitions and turned to journalistic hackwork to make his living. He worked for such London papers as the *Literary Gazette* and the *News of Literature and Fashion,* writing both comic sketches of a topical nature and also pieces with a regional flavour based on incidents and stories from his Irish background. He became aware of the growing public interest in regional fiction, an interest stimulated by Maria Edgeworth, Walter Scott and the Banim brothers and, in 1826, he put together a collection of Irish regional stories under the title *Holland-Tide.* Having sold this to a London publisher, he was prevailed upon by William to return to Ireland in 1827. He never again settled in England and always had a detestation of the great city which had given him such a chilly reception in his early days.

He had his first great success with *The Collegians* in 1829 and went on to confirm his popularity with two other effective regional tales, *The Rivals* and *Tracy's Ambition.* In his later development, he devoted himself to historical fiction and writings of a didactically pious nature but gradually began to feel a growing distaste for the life of the professional writer. The artist in him began to go under to the moralist. He became tormented by scruples in regard to the behaviour of his fictional characters and increasingly felt that he was pointlessly occupied in the production of trivial tales while others, like his brothers, were doing worthwhile work in useful professions. His personal unhappiness was intensified by his one real love-affair. In 1829 he met Lydia Fisher, a young Quaker lady a few years his senior. She was the daughter of a well-known writer, Mary Leadbeater, and the wife of James Fisher. Griffin developed a strong attachment to Lydia but soon realised that he must stifle his love. The letters and poems which he addressed to Lydia make it quite clear that he loved her deeply but that he knew that any attempt on his part to declare his love openly would result only in misery for them both.

He appears to have considered entering the priesthood but decided against it and, in 1838, surprised his family by announcing his intention to enter the Order of the·Christian Brothers, an organisation founded some years earlier by Edmund Ignatius Rice for the education of the Catholic poor. Griffin bade farewell to his literary labours by burning most of his manuscripts and entered the Chritian Brothers' house at North Richmond Street, Dublin in September 1838. He was transferred to the Order's house in

Cork, the North Monastery, in June of the following year and seems to have settled down to his new life with characteristic conscientiousness. He abandoned writing altogether and seems to have done so with relief, giving himself instead to his teaching and devotional duties. In 1840, he contracted typhus fever and died, after a short illness, in June of that year. His grave, marked by a simple headstone inscribed 'Brother Gerald Joseph Griffin' and giving his age as thirty six years, can still be seen in the little community cemetery at the North Monastery in Cork.

THE COLLEGIANS

After a short and bitter experience of the London theatre of the 1820s, Gerald Griffin abandoned his early dreams of success as a dramatist and began to turn to the writing of regional fiction. His first journalistic pieces were in this vein, drawing upon his memories of his native province of Munster. Indeed, he gave his first series of essays in the *Literary Gazette* the rather ponderous Latin title, *Horae Monomienses* ('Monomia' being the ancient name for the province of Munster). He was aware that there was an audience for such work, an audience created by such well-known older contemporaries as Maria Edgeworth with *Castle Rackrent*, Scott with the 'Waverley' novels and the brothers Banim who had a success with the first series of *Tales by the O'Hara Family* in 1825. It was understandable that Griffin's thoughts should turn to the writing of fiction of a similar kind as he shed his hopes of making a success on the stage. His letters home, which had at first been full of his visits to various London theatres and details of dramatic plots with which he was experimenting, now began to change in tone and reflect his new interest in prose fiction, both novels and short stories. In 1826 he wrote to his family in Limerick to ask them to furnish him with materials which he might work up into story form:

> At present I am working up my recollections to furnish a book which I shall call 'Munster Anecdotes', ... My anecdotes are all short stories, illustrative of manners and scenery precisely as they stand in the south of Ireland, never daring to travel out of perfect and easy probability. Could you not send me materials for a few short tales, laying the scene about the sea-coast—Kilkee? Novelty at least. Reality you know is all the rage now.

This is a voice which will become familiar in Irish letters, the voice of the literary exile in search of materials from his native place. Nearly a century later we hear the same note from another ambitious young exile, who was to pester his friends and relatives for the materials which would feed his great monster of a book, *Ulysses*. The first fruits of Griffin's labours as a writer of regional fiction appeared in 1827, when he published a collection of Irish tales under the title, *Holland-Tide*. He was soon to base his best-known work, *The Collegians*, not on any tale passed on to him at second-hand by members of his family but on a notorious incident which had shocked the countryside while he was still in his teens, long before he had taken his playwriting ambitions to London in the first place. This was what was to become known as the 'Colleen Bawn' murder. If reality was indeed 'all the rage', as Gerald had averred in his letter home, there was reality aplenty to be found in the story of this brutal killing on which Griffin was to base one of the most famous of Irish romantic novels, a work which was later to produce in turn a highly popular melodrama in Dion Boucicault's *The Colleen Bawn* and a much-loved opera in Benedict's *The Lily of Killarney*. The fact that the novel was to be made the basis of two highly successful stage works may well be traced back to Griffin's love for the drama and his habit of writing into his novels scenes of strong dramatic content which lent themselves easily to adaptation for the stage.

The real-life story burst on the public attention on the morning of 6 September, 1819, when the body of a young girl was washed ashore at Moneypoint on the River Shannon. The body was in an advanced state of decomposition but was eventually identified through dental evidence as that of Ellen Hanley who had run away from her home near Croom, Co. Limerick, in the previous June. Her seducer was one John Scanlan, son of a leading county family and recently a lieutenant in the Royal Marines. Scanlan had gone through a mock marriage with Ellen who was barely sixteen and the pair had disappeared from view, taking with them the small savings of Ellen's uncle and guardian. Scanlan was hunted down, arrested and brought to trial for the murder. In a desperate effort to save him, his family briefed Daniel O'Connell for the defence and the move almost succeeded. So ably did O'Connell plead on his client's behalf that he at first swayed the jury into disagreeing about their verdict but Scanlan was eventually convicted and condemned to death. The day after the verdict had been delivered, O'Connell privately made it quite clear that he was in no doubt of his client's guilt. He wrote in a letter to his wife:

> This is a *good* assizes. You will, however, be surprised to hear that I had a client convicted yesterday for a murder for whom I fought a hard battle and yet I do not feel any the most slight regret at his conviction. It is very unusual with me to be *so* satisfied, but he is a horrid villain. In the first place he got a creature, a lovely creature of fifteen, to elope with him from her uncle who brought her up an orphan and to rob him of his all, 100 guineas, and in three weeks after he contrived to get her into a boat on the Shannon with his servant, said when he returned to Glin that he left her at Kilrush, then reported she had gone off with a sea captain, and she was not heard of afterwards for near two months when a mutilated carcase floated on shore, or rather was thrown, which was identified to be hers from some extremely remarkable teeth. He will be hanged tomorrow unless being a gentleman prevents him.

Scanlan's rank proved of no avail and he was hanged on 16 March, 1820. Subsequently, his boatman, Stephen Sullivan, whom Scanlan had accused of the murder, was also brought to trial and hanged for the crime. Sullivan admitted his guilt but claimed that Scanlan had planned the killing. It may have been from the counter-accusations of the two assassins that Griffin got the idea for the crucial exchanges in his novel between Hardress Cregan and Danny Mann, with Danny's dangerous reference to 'the glove that fits too tight' and Hardress's fatal response to this later when he gives the glove to Danny as a token that he is to dispose of Eily. At any rate, Griffin, who may actually have reported the trial of Scanlan for a Limerick newspaper, must have been profoundly affected by the horrific story of the brutal murder of the young peasant girl by her gentry lover and, ten years later, he built around this violent and sordid story the novel by which his memory principally endures. In *The Collegians,* John Scanlan becomes the romantic and passionate lover, Hardress Cregan. His bride-victim is renamed Eily O'Connor and the sinister boatman becomes the hunch-back, Danny Mann. The novel combines Griffin's interest in social realism with his enduring fondness for histrionics (a hangover, this, from his earlier passion for the stage) and the book, which was to become one of the most popular Irish novels of the century, turns into a powerful fusion of its two elements, social realism and romantic melodrama.

This was Griffin's first full-length novel. After *Holland-Tide* he had published *Tales of the Munster Festivals* which contained three stories of novella length. These had sold reasonably well but some of the reviewers had suggested that the tales showed signs of having been put into print rather hastily. Griffin, upset by these comments, found it difficult to settle into his next project. Writing to his father at this time he describes how 'I wrote half a volume of one thing and threw it by, and a volume and a half of another and threw it by also; but the third time (as they say in the Arabian Nights) I was more successful in satisfying myself'. In the event, he appears to have begun work on *The Collegians* towards the end of the summer of 1828. He had arranged with his publishers that the new work, which was to be the second series of 'tales of the Munster Festivals', should be ready in November but he failed to meet this deadline because of his several false starts. The result was that the new novel was eventually produced under considerable pressure and this fact may, for reasons which will emerge, have been greatly to its advantage. His brother, Daniel, who was with him in London at the end of 1828, describes vividly in his biography how a messenger would appear each morning at the door of their lodging with the cry 'Printers want more copy, sir' and would then be handed the manuscript of the previous day 'without revision, correction or further ceremony'. In this manner, the work was pressed quickly to a conclusion and appeared in 1829. It was to prove Griffin's most successful and popular work, earning him the substantial sum of £800, the bulk of which he is said to have sent as a gift to his parents in America.

In spite of the haste with which, according to Daniel Griffin, the novel was finally committed to paper, it is a work of leisurely amplitude rather than compression. One has the feeling that the writer, hitherto constrained by the short story form, welcomes the opportunity to work on a larger canvas which affords him adequate space to include many examples of the sort of *genre* scene which he clearly enjoyed writing and which he must have seen as altogether appropriate to the socially dogmatic purpose of his fiction as it related to his English readers. His three years in London had impressed upon him the sad and seemingly perennial fact that the English, when they bothered to think about Ireland at all, saw the neighbouring island as a morass of potential trouble-makers, a colony full of inferior beings given to periodic bursts of insurrection against their long-suffering English masters. Griffin was always consciously working to eradicate this stereotype, to bring home to the English reading public his conviction that the Irish people were capable of responding generously to benign government and that they were, by nature, both peace-loving and generous of spirit.

He was to declare his intentions explicitly in a note to a later work, *The Rivals and Tracy's Ambition,* which constituted the third in his series of 'tales of the Munster Festivals'. In the note he contrasted his own fictions with those of the Banims, to indicate that where they depicted the more turbulent side of Irish life, he himself endeavoured to put before the public a gentler version of his country and its people. Thus, *The Collegians* abounds in elaborate domestic scenes of a genial or pathetic nature. It is an intensely social novel, informed by its obligation to illustrate all levels of society obtaining in the Ireland of its day. It differs notably in this respect from fiction of the exclusively 'Big House' kind, in which the authors are generally concerned with Irish society only at its two extremes. Griffin, clearly, works very hard to enrichen and amplify the public's sense of the complexity and density of the social fabric of Ireland. He is, for example, constantly at pains to insist on the existence of an Irish, Catholic middle-class and on the moral significance of this class. They are represented in *The Collegians* by the Daly family to whose domestic affairs he devotes two chapters early in the novel.

It is sometimes suggested, not unreasonably perhaps, that in the Dalys Griffin is depicting a family similar to his own and that Mr Daly may be a fairly accurate portrait of the novelist's father, Patrick Joseph Griffin, who emerges from Daniel's biography as a genial, Micawber-like figure who was to fail with great amiability at most of the enterprises he undertook and finally seek refuge in the usual Irish economic solution of emigration to America. In his elaborate presentation of the Daly family, however, Griffin is engaged in something more than affectionate autobiography. He is very deliberately building into his novel a stable, Catholic, middle-class group whose homely virtues are intended to contrast significantly with the reckless irresponsibility of the 'half-sirs' such as Hyland Creagh and Hepton Connolly. It is from this respectable background that the sober and virtuous Kyrle Daly, who counterpoints the reckless and glamorous Hardress Cregan, will emerge to represent the virtues of the faithful and constant lover as opposed to the more hazardous attractions of the doomed hero.

There is a sense in which the Irish novel can be said to be constantly in search of a stable middle-class which has often been denied it by the turbulent nature of Irish history. Nineteenth-century England offered writers like Dickens, Jane Austen and Thackeray a society clearly stratified into lower, middle and upper classes, each knowing its place in the scheme of things and all informed by appropriate Protestant orthodoxies in matters of belief and outlook on life. Irish novelists from Griffin to Joyce, from Carleton to Kate O'Brien, have had to struggle to present an emergent Catholic middle-class through fictional conventions appropriate to another country and another range of beliefs. The depiction of solid, bourgeois stability in an exclusively

Catholic setting assumes for these writers a vital importance. It is no accident that Joyce, even after he had sweated off most of the fat from *Stephen Hero,* still elected to retain in the new and skeletal book, *A Portrait of the Artist as a Young Man,* the marvellously rich Christmas-dinner scene at the beginning. Griffin's depiction of the Daly family may err on the side of sentimentality, so anxious is he to provide a picture of an Irish Catholic family going about its respectable domestic business, but Mr Daly and Mr Dedalus are related figures and the topics under discussion in the two scenes are similar. Mr Daly affectionately hears his children's lessons as they parade before him in order of seniority. Mr Dedalus pronounces on the desirability of having his boy educated by the Jesuits. In both novels, the early scene, carefully set in fire-lit comfort with plenty of rich food on the tables, is made an important vantage-point. The social decline of the Dedalus family with its embarassing series of moonlight flittings runs through *A Portrait* and forms a vital part of its pattern of change and decline. The scene is echoed again and again in the course of the novel. It comes to mind painfully, for example, when Stephen watches his brothers and sisters sitting around a table in another, poorer house, drinking from jam-jars and singing plaintive songs.

Where Joyce uses his important early scene of domestic comfort for a complex variety of purposes which are intimately related to the symbolic patterning of the work, Griffin employs his two long chapters on the Daly household to provide a focus on the levels of society above the middle-class Dalys. The love-sick Kyrle Daly is about to set out to offer his wooden hand in marriage to Anne Chute and Mr Daly senior is made to rally him with heavy jocosity on the subject of young lovers generally. Then he proceeds to recount comic stories about the Chute and Cregan families which are clearly intended to bring their social pretensions down a peg or two. Mr Daly's first story is about Mrs Chute's robust wooing of her second husband. Left a widow, the amazonian Hetty Trenchard literally whipped little Tom Chute into marrying her, acording to Mr Daly's amused account of the matter. Kyrle can scarcely credit that the whip-wielding Hetty of his father's tale has turned into the kind old lady who is now the elegant and respected chatelaine of Castle Chute and the mother of his beloved Anne.

His father's second story is at the expense of the Cregans. We see once again that Griffin is writing with his eye on a foreign audience when we are told that the Cregans behaved 'in a manner that might make an Englishman smile'. Mr Daly takes for granted the amusement of an hypothetical English listener, as he tells the belittling story of the Cregans' purchase of a showy mausoleum in the local churchyard. Daniel Corkery, in the opening chapter of his *Syngé and Anglo-Irish Literature,* while granting that Griffin's work lives by what he calls 'Irish suffrage', nevertheless accuses him of being 'the type of the non-Ascendancy writer who under the stress of the literary moulds of his time wrote Colonial literature'. Throughout *The Collegians* one can discern Griffin's faintly uneasy sense that he is depicting an Ireland which must frequently strike the English reader as strange. The norms of social judgement are English norms and, judged by them, the Cregans' vulgarity would be appropriately placed. In *The Collegians* social stability belongs with the middle-class Dalys and the Cregans are a rackety and pretentious set of half-sirs. Later in the novel, two chapters will also be devoted to domestic scenes of a very different kind in the Cregan household when the drunken violence of the profligate Hyland Creagh and Hepton Connolly very nearly results in the death of Hardress Cregan himself. The drunken and violent scenes in Chapters XVII and XVIII are clearly meant to contrast with the well-mannered homeliness of Chapters 111 and IV, just as the sober, dependable Kyrle Daly is intended as a foil to the excitable, unreliable Hardress.

The Collegians opens with a carefully orchestrated evocation of a bygone age, an age of lost innocence, a paradisal era set quite literally in a garden, since Garryowen, the scene of the action, has an Irish name which means 'Owen's garden'. About fifty years earlier, we are told, Garryowen served the neighbouring city of Limerick as a convenient holiday resort, 'presenting accommodations similar to those which are offered to the London mechanic by the Battersea tea-gardens'. Griffin, so recently returned from London, has his eye firmly on his English readers and is at pains to establish his Limerick setting in terms to which they can easily relate from their own city. Equally, of course, this method has the further effect of aggrandising Limerick itself, making it seem an urban centre of importance rather than a minor provincial town. Griffin's description of his lost 'Auburn' recalls his great fondness for Goldsmith and his familiarity with *The Deserted Village*:

> The old people drank together under the shades of trees—the young played at ball, goal, or other athletic exercises on the green; while a few lingering by the hedge-rows with their fair acquaintances, cheated the time with sounds less boisterous, indeed, but yet possessing their fascination also.

It is in this lost rural paradise that Griffin sets his story, moving back in time half a century from his own day and identifying the period of the novel's events for us quite specificially. As Eily's father sits at his front door, he is made to 'discourse of the politics of the day—of Lord Halifax's administration—of the promising young patriot, Mr Henry Grattan—and of the famous Catholic concessions of 1773'. This careful focussing of the novel's period is surely not without some historical overtones of an ironic kind. Catholic Emancipation was eventually to be grudgingly granted in the very year of the publication of *The Collegians,* 1829, and the long gap of almost sixty years which lay between the first small concessions to Catholics and O'Connell's eventual victory had been a period of blighted hopes for the majority of the Irish people. It had seen the brief, glamorous efflorescence of 'Grattan's Parliament', the unsuccessful effort of the Irish 'Protestant Nation' to identify itself, and the cynical corruption of Pitt's Union policies. It had also seen the beginnings of concessions to the majority religion and the bloody extinction of the '98 insurrection. It had witnessed the decline of Grattan and the rise of O'Connell. Griffin is looking back to the beginnings of the second half of the eighteenth century in Ireland, to a time of delusive promise, across a great divide of political bitterness and disappointment. It is not surprising that his depiction of the ruined Garryowen of his own day contrasts so bleakly with its earlier jocund splendours:

> The still notorious suburb is little better than a heap of rubbish, where a number of smoked and mouldering walls, standing out from the masses of stone and mortar, indicate the position of a once populous row of dwelling-houses. A few roofs yet remain unshaken, under which some impoverished families endeavour to work out a wretched subsistence, by maintaining a species of huxter trade, by cobbling old shoes, and manufacturing ropes. A small rookery wearies the ears of the inhabitants at one end of the outlet, and a rope-walk, which extends along the adjacent slope of Gallows-green (so called for certain reasons), brings to the mind of the conscious spectator associations that are not calculated to enliven the prospect. Neither is he thrown into a more jocular frame of mind as he picks his steps over the insulated paving stones that appear amid the green slough with which the street is deluged, and encounters, at the other end, an alley of coffin-makers' shops, with a fever hospital on one side and a churchyard on the other. A person who was bent on a journey to the other world could not desire a more expeditious outfit than Garryowen could now afford him, nor a more commodious choice of conveyances, from the machine on the slope above glanced at, to the pest-house at the farther end.

As Thomas Flanagan has pointed out, Griffin crams his opening pages with ominous symbols of death. This tale of the ruin of an innocent is set in an Auburn which will itself lose its innocence and Griffin fills it with portents of doom. It is now a grim place, which manufactures ropes and coffins. There is a Gallows-green nearby and a fever-hospital confronts a churchyard. Over it all sounds the grating cry of birds of ill-omen. Eily O'Connor is to begin her adventures in a village marked, as she is herself, for destruction, and whose brief period of carefree living will quickly founder just as her own heady *affaire* with Hardress Cregan will soon come to a grim conclusion also. Griffin assigns her the feast-day of the national saint, 17 March, as her birthday. If we were dealing with a later novelist, we would feel little hesitation in deducing that Eily symbolises a kind of national innocence which is to be made the pathetic victim of cruel abuse by those above her in the social scale. We are entitled to feel that Griffin is entering a genuine historical indictment here.

He is careful, in his early depiction of Eily, to present her as belonging completely to her peasant background and also as a suitable bride for Hardress. Thus, her peasant speech, which will later prove such a grave embarrassment to her lover, is amusingly described here almost as one of her attractions. We are told that 'she sometimes purloined a final letter from the King's adjectives, and prolonged the utterance of a vowel beyond the term of prosodaical orthodoxy', but 'the tongue that did so seemed to move on silver wires'. Her gentle manner hides 'the traces of a harsh and vulgar education' but the harshness and vulgarity have been mitigated somewhat by the teaching imparted to her by her uncle, Father Edward, a cultured priest who has attended the university of Salamanca. It is only when Father Edward leaves the district that Eily abandons the quiet and orderly existence she has hitherto led, begins to affect gay apparel and goes about to dances and other rural jollifications. She rejects her local suitors, Foxy Dunat the hair-cutter, Mr Daly's ill-favoured servant Lowry Looby, and even the principal suitor, Myles Murphy, who will figure largely later in the story. Her contact with Hardress and his hunchback boatman begins romantically enough when Hardress comes to the rescue of Mihil O'Conor and Eily when they are being molested by a boisterous crowd of Patrick's Day revellers. After this, Danny Mann acts as go-between for the lovers while seeming merely to visit the O'Connor home to purchase ropes from Mihil. Eily's secret marriage to Hardress is cleverly hinted at as early as the end of Chapter II and she then disappears from view and is not glimpsed again until the Dalys, looking out on the river at breakfast-time, see Hardress's boat skimming by with the mysterious, blue-cloaked figure which we know to be Eily hidden under her hood. This moving of Eily into the background of the narrative is one of the novel's more effective tactics and in this, one feels, Griffin is being true to the real-life story which was his model, conveying through his tactful treatment of Eily much of the poignancy of the lonely and terrible death of her prototype, Ellen Hanley. Eily lingers in the background for a good deal of the novel, her presence often conveyed to us only by the thoughts of Hardress or the conversations and speculations of others. Her pale shade haunts the book's many lively scenes, remaining in the background as an innocent reproach which is all the more effective for being generally silent.

Kyrle Daly's wooing of Anne Chute takes us quickly to Castle Chute where, in Chapters VIII and IX, Griffin expands his novel's canvas by presenting to us most of the novel's cast, in the form of visitors to the castle. We are admitted to the castle by 'an old portress, talking Irish', a detail not without some significance in view of the amusing play which Griffin will later make with the cunning bilingualism of some of his peasant characters. We are now to encounter the gentry playing host to a mixed company of Irish and English visitors and Griffin always revels in acting as observer and interpreter of such encounters. His three years' experience as a busy London journalist combine with his affectionate interest in the linguistic nuances of his own locality to set going a richly varied pattern of revealing conversation. We hear, for example, Dr Lucas Leake in conversation with Captain Gibson of the local garrison and the encounter between the two is made the occasion for some mildly ironic historical comedy:

71

The rosy and red-coated Captain Gibson, who was a person of talent and industry in his profession, was listening with much interest to Doctor Lucas Leake, who possessed some little antiquarian skill in Irish remains, and who was at this moment unfolding the difference which existed between the tactics of King Lugh-Lamh-Fada, and those issued from his late most gracious Majesty's War-Office; between one of King Malachy's hobbilers and a life-guardsman; between an English halberd and a stone-headed gai-bulg, and between his own commission of lieutenant and the Fear Comhlan Caoguid of the Fion Erin.

Dr Leake's enthusiastic explanations of the distinctions between the military techniques of ancient Ireland and those of her modern conqueror, presented to a courteous but puzzled Captain Gibson, offer an amused side-glance at the mutual incomprehension of centuries. The scene recalls, in some sense, Maria Edgeworth's elaborate treatment of Count O'Halloran in *The Absentee*.

We are now introduced at length also to Myle-na-Copaleen, Myles of the Ponies, who appears before the assembled company to beg for the release of his horses from the pound where they have been imprisoned by the surly steward, Dan Dawley, for straying. Griffin obviously delights in presenting this figure, in whom he combines a sort of Arcadian simplicity with great natural dignity. Myles is made to flatter everyone present and eventually succeeds in insinuating that he is related to all of them however distantly and his engaging combination of forthright honesty with supple-tongued compliment wins the hearts of his amused listeners who promptly grant him the release of his ponies, to the fury of Dan Dawley. The steward is angry at the mountaineer's success but Myles turns the tables on him by claiming relationship with him too. This scene in the castle, the setting of so much of the action of the novel, bustles with life. Barnaby Cregan animatedly engages Mrs Chute in conversation about his passion, cock-fighting. Hyland Creagh is twitted by Anne as he pays elderly court to her. Kyrle watches his opportunity to propose marriage to Anne. This group, also, is made to speculate about the identity of the blue-cloaked figure in Hardress's boat. As Kyrle has ridden towards the castle, he has actually seen the showy Hardress fire off a gun in salute to the castle and has heard the report of the gun fired in reply from the castle. Like the Dalys earlier, the assembled company in Castle Chute are chattering about Hardress and his mysterious companion. In the meantime, we have seen the distracted Mihil O'Connor in desperate and futile search for his missing daughter and have watched Myles-na-Copaleen in deep conversation with Lowry Looby about the girl, but as yet nobody has linked Eily with the blue-cloaked figure in the boat with Hardress.

When the company leaves the castle, it is to go to the races on the sands nearby. Along the way, Kyrle Daly proposes marriage to Anne Chute and is gently but firmly rejected by her so that he is in poor form for the excitements of the race-course. Nevertheless, he and Anne cast off their cares and proceed to introduce Captain Gibson to the peculiar delights of an Irish 'stageen' race. The Captain again plays his part here as the English observer being introduced to the humours of Irish life and the contrast once more is with the more orderly assemblies which are to be found in his native England:

> Captain Gibson ... could not, with the recollections of Ascot and Doncaster fresh in his mind, refrain from a roar of laughter at almost every object he beheld; at the condition of the horses; the serious and important look of the riders; the *Teniers* appearance of the whole course; the band, consisting of a blind fiddler with a piece of *listing* about his waist and another about his old hat; the self-importance of the stewards, Tim Welsh, the baker, and Batt Kennedy, the poet *janius* of the village, as they went in a jog trot round the course, collecting shilling subscriptions to the saddle from all who appeared on horseback.

Anne Chute appoints herself his guide to the scene and embarks upon a lengthy and jocose account of the village jockeys and their mounts, all done in a sort of mocking, sub-Vergilian syntax of a kind which foreshadows Griffin's more effective comedy in the celebrated hedge-school scene in a subsequent novel, *The Rivals*. Griffin's awareness of his English audience often intrudes rather obviously at this point but when he turns to describing the stageen race itself his prose leaps into life and all the self-conscious ornamentation disappears:

> The blacksmith's grey horse started at a heap of sea-weed, and suffered the nailer's mare to come down like a thunder-bolt upon his haunches. Both steeds fell, and the process-server, who rode on their heels, falling foul of them as they lay kicking on the sand, was compelled to share in their prostration. This accident produced among the fallen heroes a series of kicks and bruises, in which the horses were not idle. O'Reilly, clinching his hand, hit the nailer a straightforward blow between the eyes, which so effectually interfered with the exercise of those organs that he returned the favour with a powerful thrust in the abdomen of his own prostrate steed. For this good office he was rewarded by the indignant quadruped with a kick over the right ear, which made it unnecessary to inflict a second, and the quarrel remained between the process-server and the blacksmith, who pummelled one another as if they were pounding flax, and with as much satisfaction as if they had never got drunk together in their lives. They were at length separated and borne from the ground, all covered with blood and sand, while their horses with much difficulty were set upright on their legs, and led off to the neighbouring slope.

Various perceptive critics have noted Griffin's idiomatic unease, which is so clearly to be seen in this area of the novel. Edith Somerville, reviewing a re-issue of *The Collegians* in 1920, made rich fun at the expense of Griffin's laborious dialogue and quoted delightedly the pompous Kyrle Daly's plea to Anne Chute when she refuses his proposal of marriage: 'Let me implore you to recall that hasty negative' mouths the unhappy suitor. Edith Somerville is suitably caustic, remarking that 'it was the convention of Griffin's period that the higher the birth the taller the talk', but she makes large claims for Griffin's command of the vigorous peasant idiom which he assigns to such characters as Lowry Looby, Poll Naughten and Dalton, the dying huntsman whom we encounter in Chapter XVII. She prefers Griffin's command of such idiom to Carleton's and appears surprised at her own judgement in this matter, remarking that Carleton was himself a peasant while Griffin 'came of a family of good standing and education'. Donald Davie was to pursue a similar line of comment when he came to consider Griffin in the context of his study of Scott. He found 'a yawning gulf between the vitality of the peasants' brogue and the frigidity of the more genteel dialogue'. Griffin's style, he contends, is 'always excessive' and he goes on to describe some of Griffin's elaborate descriptive prose as 'babu's English'. He recognises, however, that 'Griffin's is a case that calls for special pleading, just as the babu's does' and suggests that in Griffin we see 'an un-English mind trying to express itself in a language wholly foreign to its most intimate habits of thought and feeling'. James Joyce was to crystallise the dilemma in the bitter reflections of Stephen Dedalus in the course of his encounter with the Prefect of Studies in Chapter V of *A Portrait of the Artist as a Young Man:*

> The language in which we are speaking is his before it is mine. How different are the words *home, Christ, ale, master,* on his lips and on mine! I cannot speak or write these words without unrest of spirit. His language, so familiar and so foreign, will always be for me an acquired speech. I have not made or accepted its words. My voice holds them at bay. My soul frets in the shadow of his language.

The fact is that Griffin had always quite deliberately worked in a wide variety of idioms, right from his early days in London. A comparison of the work he did for the *Literary Gazette* with what he wrote for the *News of Literature and Fashion* reveals this at once. The first sketches he sold to the *Gazette* were all of a regional nature and he introduced the first of them to his English audience with a revealing prefatory remark:

> I have been enabled to procure some instances which are current amongst the peasantry of the South of Ireland, in their vernacular tongue; and I shall venture to subjoin a few, almost literally rendered into English.

This shows him in the role of self-appointed interpreter of a Gaelic-speaking people and an emergent Anglo-Irish. His sketches for the *News,* however, were altogether different. In them he was offering reviews of contemporary theatrical performances, jocose pieces on comic events of the day and, occasionally, serious moral comment on matters of English interest. In these sketches, Griffin invariably discards his Irish *persona* completely and plays the part of an English journalist writing for an English public. Long before he embarked upon *The Collegians,* he had confronted the Anglo-Irish writer's principal dilemma, the creation of an idiom, and had ended as most Anglo-Irish writers do by creating several. Regrettably, his more solemn passages undoubtedly have a tendency to lapse into periphrastic pseudo-Augustanisms and cumbersome circumlocutions so that he seems at times to be trying to write very bad Goldsmith. Nevertheless, where his genuine interest is engaged his formal idiom can often be plain and effective and his peasant dialogue is almost invariably lively and entertaining, as Edith Somerville, herself no mean practitioner, was quick to acknowledge.

Unfortunately, some of Griffin's more tedious formulations are brought to bear on what is, perhaps, the most important chapter in the first half of the novel, Chapter XIII, in which Kyrle Daly and Hardress Cregan have an extended discussion on their sharply contrasting social attitudes, a discussion which is of central importance to our understanding of Hardress's character and the entire development of the plot. It is inevitable that when these two 'collegians' get together 'high talk' should be the order of the day and Griffin's own awareness of the risks he runs with this chapter are indicated by its cumbersome title, 'How the Two Friends Hold a Longer Conversation Together Than the Reader May Probably Approve'. Hardress is here made to expose to us those facets of his character which have made him reject Anne Chute and marry Eily.

It emerges that the handsome and dashing Hardress is not at ease in society and he explains his inadequacies to his companion by professing a love for what he terms 'simplicity' and a detestation for the opposing quality which he terms 'elegance'. By this he means those social conventions which he sees as mere affectations. A lengthy argument ensues, with Hardress taking the side of 'simplicity' and Kyrle the spokesman for the forms and conventions of society. In this verbal battle between sense and sensibility it rapidly appears that Hardress once felt warm affection for Anne Chute but that he was repelled by a certain elegant reserve in her manner and so deeply resented her apparent coldness to him that he tells Kyrle that she received him as if he were 'a tax-gatherer or a travelling dancing-master'. Hardress passionately professes his fondness for all that is natural and unaffected in preference to all that is fashionable, elegant and cultivated:

> 'As I prefer the works of nature to the works of man, the fresh river breeze to the dusty and smoky zephyr of Capel Street, the bloom on a cottage cheek to the crimson japan that blazes at the Earl of Buckinghamshire's drawing-rooms; as I love a plain beef-steak before a grilled attorney, this excellent whisky-punch before my mother's confounded currant-wine, and anything else that is pure and natural before anything else that is adulterated and artificial; so do I love the wild hedge-flower, simplicity, before the cold and sapless exotic, fashion; so do I love the voice of affection and of nature before that of finesse and affectation.

His companion opposes him at all points, warns him that he is still very young, and that as he matures in society he will find it advisable to conform to its conventions. In reply, Hardress shamefacedly admits that he is troubled by some sort of social timidity which inhibits him in company but he tries hard to explain this away. It is not, he contends, anything as ignoble as mere cowardice. Rather is it the case that he is sickened by the 'solemn folly of bows, and becks, and wreathed smiles that can be put on or off at pleasure'. Kyrle tries to tutor his touchy friend on the usefulness of the common forms of society and their function in keeping the wheels of social exchange oiled and smooth-running but the reader knows, and this is the chapter's most effective and pervasive irony, that Hardress has already put his dangerously over-simplified principles into action by marrying his 'wild hedge flower', Eily. Sadly, Kyrle Daly is quite right in his prophecy that Hardress will live to regret his over-simplified romanticism. It is what sets him on his path to destruction.

Griffin was always fascinated by the sort of excessive commitment to 'simplicity' which he depicts in Hardress Cregan. He had already written a very effective short story about just such a character, Eugene Hamond of *The Half-Sir,* one of the three stories which make up *Tales of the Munster Festivals.* He was to return to the type in his long, historical novel, *The Invasion,* with the character of the Saxon, Kenric. Furthermore, the eponymous hero of the only work which he preserved when he burned his manuscipts in 1838, the play *Gisippus,* is just such a person. Hardress Cregan is, in fact, merely the most outstanding example in a long line of such 'sensitives' and Griffin's interest in such figures is the source of the psychological insight he displays in his handling of them in his fiction. He traces with considerable skill the gradual alteration in Hardress's feelings towards Anne and the consequent changes in his attitude to Eily. He shows how Hardress soon begins to regret his haste in forming an alliance with someone who, however simple and unspoilt, is nevertheless his social inferior and likely to prove a social embarrassment among his friends. In Chapter XX, Hardress's unease is finely conveyed and his dilemma cruelly exposed. The drunken Poll Naughten, Eily's guardian in her cottage hide-out and effectively her gaoler, is shown confronting the lovers and demanding money for drink. She is already drunk and when Hardress pompously reprimands her by telling her that her young mistress 'would not become a participator in the sin of your drunkenness', he draws down upon himself and his bride the fury of the drunken virago who cruelly reminds him that her 'mistress' is no better than herself:

'My mistress! The rope-maker's daughter! *My* mistress! Eily-na-thiadrucha! Welcome from Gallows Green, my mistress! The poor silly crathur! Is it because I call you, with the blood of all your fathers in your veins, a gentleman, my masther, that I'd call her a lady and my misthress?'

The disparity in their stations to which Poll so crudely draws attention now begins to trouble Hardress so much that it haunts even his dreams. In a perceptive passage, Griffin has him dream that Eily has disgraced him in the company of his friends:

He dreamed that the hour had come in which he had to introduce his bride to his rich and fashionable acquaintances, and that a large company had assembled at his mother's cottage to honour the occasion. Nothing, however, could exceed the bashfulness, the awkwardness, and the homeliness of speech and accent, with which the rope-maker's daughter received their compliments; and to complete the climax of his chagrin, on happening to look round upon her during dinner, he saw her in the act of peeling a potato with her fingers! This phantom haunted him for half the night.

Griffin crystallises all of his hero's growing distaste for his peasant bride in that coarse image of her peeling the potato with her fingers. Soon, Hardress is launched on the double life which will be the ruin of him, visiting Eily in her secluded cottage but always returning to the society of Anne Chute and the gay social whirl of balls and outings which form his public life now. His attentions to Anne deceive even his mother, who attempts to bring the two of them together in marriage and is deeply angered when Hardress confesses that he is 'engaged' to another woman. His mother insists he must break this 'engagement' since his affection for Anne is by now public knowledge. Gradually, Hardress turns against Eily. She begins to upbraid him for keeping her hidden away and reminds him of the promise he made her that he would introduce her to his family. Maddened by her pleas and by his growing hatred for her, he reveals his predicament to his hunchback servant and has with him the fateful conversation about the glove which 'fits too tight'. Danny Mann admonishes him to 'take the knife to the glove'. At first, Hardress is filled with fury by the suggestion of violence against Eily and almost strangles his tempter in his rage. Soon, however, driven to desperation by his growing passion for Anne, he seeks out the hunchback, plucks off his glove, throws it to Danny and tells him his mind is altered. Although he warns his servant not to harm Eily, he also speaks so fiercely of the need to get rid of her that his remarks are open to easy misinterpretation. The novel now enters its most melodramatic phase. Danny, in obedience to his master's instructions, takes Eily from the cottage on the pretence of returning her to her father. Hardress rushes through a night of storm, arrives too late at the cottage and resigns himself to his guilt. He terrifies Poll Naughten and her husband, Phil, with his insane mutterings and his disturbed sleep, so that they now begin to suspect that some evil plan is afoot. Hardress rushes away from the cottage and returns to his mother to upbraid her furiously for thrusting him into his present predicament by urging him into a betrothal with Anne. Mrs Cregan, who does not understand his ravings, now tells him of the sudden death of Kyrle Daly's mother and urges him to attend the wake at the Daly's house. Hardress's torments continue, since he meets Eily's father at the wake and must also confront Kyrle Daly who has been told of Hardress's betrothal to Anne Chute and is bitterly angry about it.

Griffin piles agony upon agony for the distracted Hardress and the tense atmosphere of concentrated melodrama would be altogether intolerable but for the seasoning Griffin applies in the way of rural comedy from such smooth-tongued entertainers as Foxy Dunat and Lowry Looby. In his preface to his 1918 edition of the novel, Padraic Colum had likened Griffin's early work to that of the young Thomas Hardy. It is certainly the case that Griffin has a Hardy-like talent for creating rustic choruses of a convincing kind which act as commentary on and light relief from the main action. The tremendous climax of the novel is attained when the hounds discover Eily's body during the hunting party organised by Hepton Connolly. The hounds uncover their dreadful quarry in a pool and Mr Warner, the magistrate, immediately initiates official enquiries into Eily's death. Hardress, after some suitably dramatic utterances about the hounds of hell who are on his own heels, rushes off to Castle Chute. The search for the murderer now begins and provides Griffin with one more splendid opportunity for Irish comedy on the grand scale before justice is finally done. This part of the novel alternates rapidly between torrid melodrama and lively fun. The most amusing scene concerns the protracted cross-examination by Mr Warner of the termagant, Poll Naughten, and her husband, Phil, in an effort to get information about the murder.

Danny Mann, who is Poll's brother, has been captured by the military and is questioned by the magistrate who finds that 'his answers were all given in the true style of Irish witnesses, seeming to evince the utmost frankness, yet invariably leaving the querist in still greater perplexity than before he put the question'. Mr Warner awaits the arrival of Poll and Phil Naughten, hoping that he may gain some information from them which will help to convict Danny. Mrs Cregan is on tenterhooks lest the cross-examination should incriminate Hardress but, in a passage which the author of *The Playboy of the Western World* would have endorsed, Griffin makes it clear that her fears are unwarranted:

> The peasantry of Ireland have, for centuries, been at war with the laws by which they are governed, and watch their operation in every instance with a jealous eye. Even guilt itself, however naturally atrocious, obtains a commiseration in their regard, from the mere spirit of opposition to a system of government which they consider as unfriendly. There is scarcely a cottage in the south of Ireland where the very circumstance of legal denunciation would not afford, even to a murderer, a certain passport to concealment and protection.

Poll Naughten arrives in a blaze of rage and begins magnificently by abusing the soldiers:

> 'Let me in!' she exclaimed in a fierce tone; 'do you want to thrust your scarlet jacket between the tree and the rind? Let me in, you tall ramrod, or I'll pull the soap and powder out of your wig. If I had you on the mountain I'd cut the pig's tail from your poll, and make a show o' you. Do, do—draw your bay'net on me, you cowardly object. It's like the white blood o' the whole of ye! I know fifty lads your size, that would think as little of tripping you up on a fair-green, as making a high-road of your powdered carcass, as I do of snapping my fingers in your face! That for your rusty bay'net, you woman's match!

However uneasy one may feel about Griffin as a stylist in some passages of the novel, it is impossible to fault him here. He is splendidly in control of the clash of idioms which takes place in the exchanges between Poll and Mr Warner, precisely because Poll is made to use language itself as her weapon against the magistrate. This is a clash between officialdom and personality, between the representative of authority and a mountainy woman who brooks no authority. Poll's ebullient replies to Mr Warner's careful questions break about him like great word-waves and finally submerge him altogether. He soon admits defeat and, at the suggestion of Captain Gibson who has been standing by scarcely able to suppress his amusement, they next call her husband, hoping to find him a more willing and timid witness than his fearsome wife. Mr Warner is in for a further shock, however, as Phil brings to bear upon him yet another weapon from the Irish linguistic armoury, the weapon of bilingualism. To begin with, he simply answers the magistrate's questions in the Irish language, thereby angering Warner:

'Come—come—English. Swear him to know whether he does not understand English. Can you speak English, fellow?'

'Not a word, plase your honour.'

A roar of laughter succeeded this escapade, to which the prisoner listened with a wondering and stupid look. Addressing himself in Irish to Mr Cregan, he appeared to make an explanatory speech which was accompanied by a slight expression of indignation.

'What does the fellow say?' asked Mr Warner.

'Why,' said Cregan, with a smile, 'he says he will admit that he couldn't *be hung in English before his face,* but he does not know enough of the language to enable him to *tell his story* in English.'

'Well, then, I suppose we must have it in Irish. Mr Houlahan, will you act as interpreter?'

The clerk, who thought it *genteel* not to know Irish, bowed, and declared himself unqualified.

'Wisha, then,' said a gruff voice at a little distance, in a dark corner of the room, 'it isn't but what you had opportunities enough of learning it. If you went for foreign parts what would they say to you, do you think, when you'd tell 'em you didn't know the language of the country where you were born? You ought to be ashamed o' yourself, so you ought.'

This speech, which proceeded from the unceremonious Dan Dawley, produced some smiling at the expense of the euphuistic secretary, after which the steward himself was sworn to discharge the duties of the office in question.

The entire passage is a brilliant dramatisation of the mutual incomprehension of two peoples. Griffin, with the peculiarly effective bi-focal vision granted him by his expatriate experience and his intimate understanding of his own people, brings vividly to life a quintessentially Anglo-Irish tangle of words, motives and evasions. Phil Naughten's engagingly precise formulation of his linguistic crux, that he, 'couldn't *be hung in English before his face,* but he does not know enough of the language to enable him to *tell his story* in

English' is a comment on the colonial experience which is both amusing and starkly revealing. Mr Houlahan, the clerk who 'thought it *genteel* not to know Irish' is a cruelly accurate touch and he does not have to wait long to be put firmly in his place by the blunt Dan Dawley. Griffin is writing magnificently here, finely in command of his material and his effects, as he always is when exploring such oppositions. He worked as a court reporter in London and Limerick and clearly listened attentively to witnesses and barristers and his fiction often shows the benefit of such experience. There is no separation of styles here, but rather a dynamic fusion of idioms to produce a distinctive blend of comedy and social insight. Griffin's avowedly didactic purposes in his fiction are effectively submerged here in his delighted creative involvement with his material.

The climax of the novel sees Hardress assisting Danny Mann to escape from his captors and Hardress himself cravenly planning, with his mother's assistance, to marry Anne Chute as soon as possible. Danny, contrary to his master's orders, fails to leave the country and Hardress meets him on the roadway with a group of country mummers. In a burst of anger, Hardress attacks Danny and beats him cruelly and the hunchback gets his revenge by informing on Hardress, confessing their double guilt. Hardress is arrested at the height of the festivities which precede his marriage to Anne, is deported for his crime but dies before he reaches his place of exile. Danny is executed for his crime and, in time, Kyrle Daly marries Anne Chute. In the closing chapter, Griffin abandons any pretence of creative fiction, professes to be merely the historian and ties up all the loose ends with scant regard to fictional probability. At times, during the climax of the action, his passion for strong scenes of a dramatic nature comes ruinously to the fore and there are clear echoes of his experiences of Shakespearean tragedy on the London stage and of the bravura acting of famous players such as Kean and Kemble in parts ranging from Hamlet to Macbeth and Coriolanus. He had worked to elevate the character of Kyrle Daly at the expense of Hardress Cregan and was to express his surprise and regret that the public would respond more warmly to the doomed hero than to his sober and worthy friend:

> 'Look at these two characters of Kyrle Daly and Hardress Cregan .... Kyrle Daly, full of high principle, prudent, amiable and affectionate; not wanting in spirit, nor free from passion; but keeping his passions under control;thoughtful, kind-hearted, and charitable; a character in every way deserving our esteem. Hardress Cregan, his mother's spoiled pet, nursed in the very lap of passion, and ruined by indulgence—not without good feelings, but for ever abusing them, having a full sense of justice and honour, but shrinking like a craven from their dictates; following pleasure headlong, and eventually led into crimes of the blackest dye, by the total absence of all self-control. Take Kyrle Daly's character in what way you will, it is infinitely preferable; Yet I will venture to say, nine out of ten of those who read the book would prefer Hardress Cregan, just because he is a fellow of high mettle, with a dash of talent about him.'

There are clear warnings here of the growing moral scrupulosity which was eventually to destroy Griffin as a writer of fiction. Even *The Collegians,* his best-known work which has kept his memory green, is marred by authorial pronouncements of a pedantically moral kind on the evident discrepancies between the two 'collegians' of the title. The book is flawed, too, by his recurring tendency to envisage his more violent climaxes as set pieces for histrionic performance. His brother tells a revealing tale in this connection:

> 'What a great deal I would give,' he said to me one evening, while his eyes kindled with the thought, 'to see Edmund Kean in that scene of Hardress Cregan at the party, just before his arrest, where he is endeavouring to do politeness to the ladies while the horrid warning voice is in his ear'.

Yet, while the novel's fustian now looks distinctly shoddy, the good, honest frieze of its genuine, rustic realism has worn quite splendidly to the present day. While Hardress rages wildly on to his inevitable doom, an entire talkative society is brought to vivid life about him in the persons of Lowry Looby, Foxy Dunat the hair-cutter, the virago Poll Naughten and the engaging Myles of the Ponies. Above these in the social scale we see the rackety half-sirs drinking and brawling on their ruinous way, in the persons of Hyland Creagh and Hepton Connolly and their ilk. The country people move convincingly before us, telling stories, recalling old legends, offering themselves to us as a principle of continuity in a turbulent and disorderly age. If Gerald Griffin, at his weakest, sometimes lapses into gothic extravagance, at his best he conveys the fabric of the Ireland of his times with a loving fidelity which has scarcely been surpassed.

Selected Bibliography

RELATED WORKS
Tales of the Munster Festivals, London, 1827.
The Rivals and Tracy's Ambition, London, 1829.
(pbk reprint, CERIUL, Université de Lille III, 1978).

BIOGRAPHY
Daniel Griffin, *Life of Gerald Griffin Esq.,* London, 1843.
Ethel Mannin, *Two Studies in Integrity,* London, 1954, 17-132.
John Cronin, *Gerald Griffin 1803-1840: A Critical Biography,* Cambridge, 1978.

CRITICAL STUDIES
Thomas Flanagan, *The Irish Novelists 1800-1850,* New York, 1959, 205-51.
Donald Davie, *The Heyday of Sir Walter Scott,* London, 1961.

CRITICAL ARTICLES
B. G. MacCarthy, 'Irish Regional Novelists of the Early Nineteenth Century', *The Dublin Magazine,* (July-Sept. 1946), 28-37.
John Cronin, 'A Select List of Works Concerning Gerald Griffin', *Irish Booklore* (August 1971), 150-6.
Benedict Kiely, 'The Two Masks of Gerald Griffin', *Studies* (Autumn 1972), 241-51.

IV

William Carleton
THE BLACK PROPHET

William Carleton 1794-1869

Carleton was born at Prillisk, Co. Tyrone, the son of a tenant-farmer. He was the youngest of fourteen children. His father's knowledge of both the Old and the New Testament and his fund of Gaelic lore were of obvious importance to the shaping of the future writer. His mother was renowned in the area as a sweet singer of songs both in Irish and in English. The boy was schooled by a succession of hedge-school teachers whose often idiosyncratic behaviour was to provide him with much material for his stories. At the age of fourteen, young Carleton decided that he would make his way to Munster as a 'poor scholar' but he got homesick along the way and had his celebrated dream of being chased by a bull, which he interpreted as an omen bidding him abandon his travels for the moment. He went back to his delighted family and stayed with them for a further five years, during which he appears to have enjoyed himself hugely, excelling at athletic contests and at dancing. In addition to pleasuring himself with sport and rural jollification, he attended a classical school at Donagh in Co. Monaghan and another in Dundalk.

When he was about nineteen he set off on a pilgrimage to Lough Derg. His father had cherished the hope that at least one of his children would become a priest but his youngest son's journey to the famous island centre of devotion had quite the opposite effect and William's gradual abandonment of Catholicism seems to date from about the time of his pilgrimage, an experience which was also to provide him with material for one of his most controversial early stories. He was eventually to abandon Catholicism and become a Protestant, a switch of religious allegiances which commentators have interpreted in various ways. W. B. Yeats took the view that Carleton remained at all times a Catholic at heart. Benedict Kiely relates his Protestantism to his ambiguous contact with Caesar Otway and sees his decisions as being based on the hard facts of poverty rather than on theological conviction:

> William Carleton scrambled up on the fence with the firm intention of
> becoming a Protestant, ended up with a long leg dangling on either side of
> the rickety division. The one advantage was that perched on the fence
> with his heels kicking the air he could work and eat.

More recently, Terence Brown has taken issue with such judgements and has presented a case for taking Carleton's Protestantism more seriously. Brown, however, concerns himself with Carleton's old age and with his friendship with various sympathetic clergymen of both denominations. One feels that the Carleton who, at the end of a long life, conversed with William Pakenham Walsh, later bishop of Ossory, was hardly the same Carleton who obliged Caesar Otway with 'exposures' of Catholic superstitions for *The Christian Examiner.*

Carleton, inspired by a reading of *Gil Blas,* finally left home for good in 1818 and set off for Dublin by a leisurely and roundabout route. Along the way, he called on the Jesuits at Clongowes and also visited Maynooth. He finally reached Dublin, almost penniless, and lived from hand to mouth until he met a Mr Fox who ran one of Erasmus Smith's schools. Through Fox, Carleton got a job as clerk in the Sunday School Office at a salary of £60 a year. He married Fox's niece, Jane Anderson, but soon found himself in financial straits once more. He was dismissed from his post in the Sunday School Office and, to keep his wife and baby son, had to take a post as teacher in a Protestant school in Mullingar. In 1825 he was back in Dublin once more and there he met Caesar Otway, one of the more able and active of the Protestant proselytisers of the time. Otway had just founded *The Christian Examiner* and he recruited Carleton to write for it. His first contribution to Otway's paper was 'A Pilgrimage to St Patrick's Purgatory' which appeared in 1828 and he continued to write for the paper until 1831. Roger McHugh has pithily characterised this phase of Carleton's career as 'graphic pen-pictures and sectarian bias laid on with a trowel'. When he broke with Otway, Carleton went on to write for other Dublin periodicals such as *The National Magazine, The Dublin Literary Gazette* and *The Dublin University Magazine.* The first series of his *Traits and Stories of the Irish Peasantry* appeared in 1830, the second in 1833. This is the work on which his literary reputation now principally rests. In it he draws on his vivid memory of his youth and pours forth a memorable series of portraits of hedge-schoolmasters, faction fighters, 'poor scholars'. dancing-masters, country fiddlers, a whole gallery of the characters he recalled from his early days in Tyrone or had met on his travels about the country. He also recorded memorably, in stories such as the fearsome *Wildgoose Lodge,* the darker and more violent aspects of the Ireland of his day.

Carleton moved on from short stories to the novel with *Fardorougha the Miser,* which was first published in serial form in *The Dublin University Magazine* and went into book form in 1839. He subsequently published upwards of a dozen more novels, including *Valentine McClutchy* (1845) and *The Emigrants of Ahadarra* (1848). The bewildering variety of the attitudes and stances he adopted is summed up for us by Thomas Flanagan:

> Before his career was run he had written for every shade of Irish opinion—stern Evangelical tracts for Caesar Otway; denunciations of the landlords for Thomas Davis; patronizing sketches for *The Dublin University Magazine*; unctuous Catholic piety for James Duffy; a few sketches for Richard Pigott, the sinister mock-Fenian who was to forge the famous Parnell correspondence. By the eighteen forties he was the most celebrated of Irish writers; ten years later he was written-out, a hack whose pen was for hire in Dublin's ugly literary wars. He had but one subject, the days of his youth and the world in which he had lived them. This is the subject which haunted him and drove his pen; to this subject he was faithful, and to nothing else.

Carleton was granted a government pension in 1848 but it was not generous enough to free him permanently from financial pressures. He went on writing to the end of his life in an effort to keep one jump ahead of his debts. He died of cancer of the tongue in Dublin in 1869, with his Autobiography still largely incomplete, and was buried in Mount Jerome cemetery.

THE BLACK PROPHET

Most readers of Irish fiction pay lip-service to the notion of Carleton's pre-eminence among the Irish novelists of the nineteenth century. Yet, very few of his works have remained in print and no definitive work of criticism has yet appeared. We have, it would seem, decided to fight shy of this flawed giant. In an article published in 1938, Roger McHugh remarked on this pattern of ardent neglect:

> If Carleton, as Charles Gavan Duffy said, "lifted a head like Slieve Donard over his contemporaries," modern surveyors of nineteenth-century Irish literature in English must suffer from defective vision; for there is little mention of him in their pages. The only biography of him, and it is not a complete biography, was brought out by D. J. O'Donoghue in 1896. So far the twentieth century has added little; sketches by Darrell Figgis and by Stephen Gwynn, a brief survey by Dr Krans, and Miss Shaw's monograph on his native district. The rest, but for an occasional academic reference, is silence; that public neglect, of which he complained, somewhat unjustly, during his life has been accorded to him in full measure since his death.

Today, some forty years later, the situation might be said to be essentially unchanged. We can add to McHugh's short list Benedict Kiely's warmly enthusiastic animation of the man and his fiction in *Poor Scholar,* Thomas Flanagan's admirable chapters in his indispensable study, *The Irish Novelists 1800-1850* and Margaret Chesnutt's recent and useful exploration of some of the short stories, but there has been no really comprehensive work which would place in perspective for us this major figure whom Yeats dubbed 'the great novelist of Ireland, by right of the most Celtic eyes that ever gazed from under the brow of story-teller.' It may well be Yeats himself who has been responsible for a certain lasting distortion in Carleton's reputation. As a very young man, Yeats delved into the Irish novelists in a commendable search for a Celtic note and came up, as one might expect, with some interesting and curious judgements. His letters indicate that he read pretty widely in the novels and stories of the early writers of the century, though his genuine enthusiasm was occasionally tempered a little both by tedium and by pressure of time. 'What a voluminous creature Carleton is', he writes with understandable impatience, in a letter to Father Russell in 1889. In the same letter he asks Fr Russell what he considers to be Banim's best work and confesses that he must take only 'a few specimen nibbles at him'. Of Carleton, however, he took more than a few specimen nibbles and he published his compilation, *Stories from Carleton,* in 1889, with an Introduction which he later confessed had been done in rather a rush to convenience his publisher at an awkward moment. It may be helpful at this point to quote a little from the youthful Yeats's hastily written but influential preface:

He is the great novelist of Ireland, by right of the most Celtic eyes that
ever gazed from under the brow of story-teller. ... There is no wistfulness
in the works of Carleton. I find there, especially in his longer novels, a
kind of clay-cold melancholy. One is not surprised to hear, great
humorist though he was, that his conversation was more mournful than
humorous. He seems, like the animals in Milton, half emerged only from
the earth and its broodings. When I read any portion of the "Black
Prophet", or the scenes with Raymond the Madman in "Valentine
M'Clutchy", I seem to be looking out at the wild, storm-clouds that lie in
heaps at sundown along the western seas of Ireland; all nature, and not
merely man's nature, seems to pour out for me its inbred fatalism.

Half a dozen years later, in a review of *The Life of William Carleton* which
Yeats contributed to *The Bookman* of March 1896, he is rather more severe,
more critically detached:

> The author of "The Traits and Stories" was not an artist, as those must
> needs be who labour with spiritual essences, but he was what only a few
> men have ever been or can ever be, the creator of a new imaginative
> world, the demiurge of a new tradition.

Later again, in 1904, Yeats wrote in John Quinn's copy of his *Stories from
Carleton* what seems, in the light of his earlier commendations, an almost
coldly dismissive comment:

> I thought no end of Carleton in those days and would still I dare say if I
> had not forgotten him.

Thus, it would seem that, as Yeats plunged ever deeper into the Celtic past, he
inevitably abandoned Carleton for Cuchulain, but his early encomia have
survived as a cogent critical influence in a manner which the older Yeats might
himself have deprecated. Those youthful enthusiasms seem to have acquired
the cachet of the mature, magisterial Yeats rather than of the young editor
who actually wrote them.

If we push back beyond Yeats in time, to seek out something closer to a
contemporary view of Carleton, we find, I think, judgements which are
perhaps closer to the modern view of his great but flawed achievements.
Patrick Joseph Murray, the biographer of John Banim, in a lengthy review
article in the *Edinburgh Review* in 1852, first sensibly sets aside some
contemporary reservations about Carleton's tiresome sectarian posturings:

> The young peasant genius was, in the very commencement of his career as
> author, patronised by some of the most unbending enemies of Catholic
> emancipation and the most noted leaders in the angry warfare of the day:
> and several of his early tales copied but too faithfully the language and
> spirit of his new political associates. All his writings, for several years
> back, are, we believe, entirely, or almost entirely, free from this taint.

Then, before proceeding to lengthy and enthusiastic comment on the genuine
merits of Carleton's best fiction, particularly in his short stories, Murray

offers a judgement on what he sees as a major defect in Carleton's work:

> He at times breaks in upon the narrative with a little lecture on the relations of landlord and tenant, the importance of education, the duty of forethought and economy, and the like. We do not mean to insinuate that these topics are not of the first importance, or that his strictures are not just and valuable; but they are out of place. ... The first rule is—stick to your story; whatever you add that is not a part of it, though ever so valuable in itself, will be an incumbrance, as a man's movements are embarrassed by a weight on the back, though it were a weight of gold. One of the merits of Mr Carleton's best tales is, that they convey their own lessons, and require no gloss. When he epitomises himself into a lecture, it is like the exquisite singing of a beautiful song followed by a drawling recitation of the words.

Few readers of Carleton would disagree with Murray's criticisms which, as we shall see, are only too applicable to large areas of *The Black Prophet*. It was an aspect of his performance which, if anything, worsened as he grew older and Murray, towards the end of this lengthy review, notices the prevalence of these traits in *The Squanders of Castle Squander,* Carleton's regrettable attempt at a 'Big House' novel, which appeared just as Murray's article was put in type. Exasperatedly, Murray concludes:

> Why will Mr Carleton persist in spoiling his stories—to say nothing of the *needless* offence given to a large portion of his readers—by dissertations on topics which any fourth-rate newspaper correspondent would handle much better than he has done, leaving that field in which he stands without an equal among the living or the dead? We write in sorrow, not in anger. He is himself a true Squander of Castle Squander, neglecting the fine gifts with which nature has endowed him, and feeding on garbage and offal.

Carleton, of course, like Griffin and the Banims, was burdened by the need to explain to his English readers the crazy political and economic system which was gradually destroying his people and, in fairness, one must grant that he is well aware himself of the disastrous effects which his extempore lectures on political economy and the land system have on the development of his fiction. In Chapter XXII of *The Black Prophet,* where he depicts Mr Travers, the magistrate, inspecting the appalling consequences of the middle-man system and its creation of hordes of pauper occupants, he feels it necessary to add an apologetic rider:

> As we are not, however, writing a treatise upon the management of property, we shall confine ourselves simply to the circumstances only of such of the tenants as have enacted a part in our narrative.

It was, in fact, quite inevitable that *The Black Prophet* would contain large quantities of the sort of tedious information which so distressed Murray. The novel is, quite literally, an occasional one, written for that most terrible of Irish occasions, the Great Hunger, and published right in the middle of that appalling national disaster. In his twenties, Carleton had witnessed the earlier famines of 1817 and 1822, terrible years the memory of which was to be eclipsed only by the greater horror which descended on the people twenty years later. Every year was, for some part of Ireland, a year of famine and the whole population lived constantly on the verge of starvation. When the potato crop failed in 1845, the authorities did not immediately take fright, since the crop had failed before, though not so extensively. Carleton published his warning novel first as a serial in the *Dublin University Magazine* where it appeared throughout 1846, by which time the full scale of the national disaster was much clearer. *The Black Prophet* was put into book form in the following year. Carleton based it on the earlier famines of 1817 and 1822 and his angry and contempuous dedication constitutes a direct impeachment of the government of the day and of preceding administrations. The Prime Minister, Lord John Russell, is directly accused of responsibility for Ireland's dreadful plight, but he is not alone:

> It is in your character of Prime Minister that I take the liberty of prefixing your Lordship's name to this "Tale of Irish Famine". Had Sir ROBERT PEEL been in office, I would have placed his name where that of your Lordship now stands. There is something not improper in this; for although I believe that both you and he are sincerely anxious to benefit our unhappy country, still I cannot help thinking that the man who in his ministerial capacity, must be looked upon as a public exponent of those principals of Government which have brought our country to her present calamitous condition, by a long course of illiberal legislation and unjustifiable neglect, ought to have his name placed before a story which details with truth the sufferings which such legislation and neglect have entailed upon our people.

The ghastly consequences of the maladministration of the country and the fatal ineptitude of governmental attempts at relief are exposed throughout the novel, which comments with particular bitterness on the astonishing fact that, even while the country starved, food was still being exported from Ireland in large quantities:

> Such indeed was the extraordinary fact! Day after day vessels laden with Irish provisions, drawn from a population perishing with actual hunger, as well as with the pestilence which it occasioned, were passing out of our ports, whilst, singular as it may seem, other vessels came in freighted with our own provisions, sent back, through the charity of England, to our relief.

Carleton's Preface to the novel, while dealing fully with the factual background to the work and his hopes that its publication would assist his unfortunate fellow-countrymen by bringing their fearsome plight to the attention of the world, also makes clear his awareness of his fictional responsibilities:

> Let not the reader imagine, however, that the principal interest of this Tale is drawn from so gloomy a topic as famine. The author trusts that the

working. of those passions and feelings which usually agitate human life
and constitute the character of those who act in it, will be found to
constitute its chief attraction.

Regrettably, Carleton's creakily melodramatic plot offers no real support to
his depiction of a famine-stricken land. His Preface had also remarked 'how
far the strongest imagery of Fiction is frequently transcended by the terrible
realities of Truth'. Ideally, the terrible realities of the truths in his novel cried
out for a sturdy plot-structure to match them and symbols grand enough to
do justice to his fearsome theme. Sadly, what he offers instead is an
unconvincing story of rural murder and mystery which is intended to
generate, in relation to the contemporary events of the novel, an atmosphere
of tension and horror. This it fails miserably to achieve. The reader soon
realises that the Black Prophet himself, Donnel Dhu, is the real guilty figure
of the piece and that Dalton has been wrongly accused of murder. In any case
we can feel little interest in ancient killings about which we know nothing
whatever. The clumsy plot concerning the tobacco-box and the re-
appearance of the supposed murder victim at the end is quite inadequate to
the maintenance of any kind of dynamic suspense and the incidents of a
contemporary nature in the work are often both sentimental and
unconvincing. Sarah's substitution of herself for Mave Sullivan in the
abduction scene falters between melodrama and farce. This general weakness
in the plot does grave disservice to the work's vitally important theme of
famine. It is not simply that the plot fails to support the theme. It positively
undermines it. Though Griffin, in *The Collegians,* often lapses into
melodramatic rant he is preserved from this sort of failure by the sustaining
background of real events involved in the 'Colleen Bawn' murder. However
lurid Hardress Cregan's utterances may become, we have the brutal murder of
Eily in our mind's eye to justify, in some sort, his ravings. Carleton's boring
twenty-year-old murder never acquires that kind of sustaining significance.
Thus, instead of underpinning the book's terrible realities, the tawdry plot
actually undercuts them, sadly diminishing the power of the novel.

Nevertheless, though the work fails to achieve an organic power, it has
intermittent flashes of Carleton's peculiar genius, both in the regions of
comedy and tragedy. The Black Prophet himself is often an impressively
ominous figure and Carleton supplies him with a splendid piece of outrageous
'prophetic' gabble early in the work:

> ... a child was born and a page was written, and an angel from heaven was
> sent to Nebbychodanazor, the prophet, who was commanded to write.
> What will I write? says Nebbychodanazor the prophet. Write down the
> fate of a faymale child, by name Mave Sullivan, daughter to Jerry
> Sullivan and his wife Bridget, of Aughnamurrin. Amin, says the prophet;
> fate is fate; what's before is not behind, neither, is what's behind before,
> and everything will come to pass that's to happen. Amin, agin, says the
> prophet, an' what am I to write?—Grandeur an' wealth—upstairs and

downstairs—silks and satins—an inside car—bracelets, earrings, and Spanish boots, made of Morroccy leather, tanned at Cordovan. Amin, agin, says Nebbychodanazor, the prophet—this is not that, neither is that the other, but everything is everything—neither can something be nothing, nor nothing something to the end of time; an' time itself is but cousin jarmin to eternity—as is recorded in the great book of fate, fortune, an' fatality.

The circumstances of the time are in themselves so terrible that they scarcely require the Prophet's grotesque verbal embroideries, as he himself indicates to Jerry Sullivan, whom he has first primed with references to the prophecies of St Columbkill:

> "Look about you, and say what is it you see that doesn't foretell famine— famine—famine! Doesn't the dark wet day, an' the rain, rain, rain, foretell it? Doesn't the rottin' crops, the unhealthy air, an' the green damp foretell it? Doesn't the sky without a sun, the heavy clouds, an' the angry fire of the West foretell it? Isn't the airth a page of prophecy, where every man may read of famine, pestilence, an' death? The airth is softened for the grave, an' in the black clouds of heaven you may see the death-hearse movin' slowly along—funeral after funeral—funeral after funeral—an' nothing to folly them but lamentation an' woe, by the widow an' orphan—the fatherless, the motherless, an' the childless—woe an' lamentation—lamentation an' woe."

Carleton is writing here with an impressive, dark power which to some extent, carries over into his portrayal of the Prophet's daughter, Sarah. She is a strange mixture of ferocity and a genuine hunger for affection. In his depiction of her angry bitterness and of her tortured relationship with her father, Carleton is groping towards the articulation of deeply meaningful implications but never quite achieving full expression. It is significant that, even at the end, when Sarah's mother has reappeared, Carleton refuses to allow this part of the plot to descend into the melodrama which besets so much of the rest of the work and makes Sarah reject the mother for whom she has so long hungered, while the mother is shown as a convincingly chilly figure in whom the warmth of natural affections has been suppressed by her experiences.

Darby Skinadre, the profiteering gombeen-man who battens on the miseries of the starving poor by hoarding meal and selling it at inflated prices during famine, is a well-realised grotesque but, unfortunately, the long scene in Chapters VI and VII where we watch him at his unpleasant dealings with his hungry customers is weakened by Carleton's regrettable lapse into sentimental melodrama with the unconvincing death of Margaret Murtagh. Furthermore, although Darby himself is sharply defined, his unfortunate victims are not individually identified for us in a manner which would evoke our compassion. Carleton, on the whole, contents himself with a parade of generic types here: 'the aged man'; 'the widower'; 'the widow—emblem of desolation and despondency'. The real possibilities of the scene are dissipated by such vapid generalities. Much more effective is Tom Dalton's fury at his beloved Margaret's death and we can believe in the angry violence with which he seizes the miserly Darby and squeezes his throat until the eyes almost pop out of his head. In fact, this novel manages to attain a genuinely convincing fictional dimension only intermittently and its most successful moments are those in which Carleton abandons his lectures and didactic moralisings and allows the narrative to explode into a distinctive kind of angry fantasy. One such moment, one of the best in the book, occurs when we meet the crazed Tom Dalton leading the terrified Darby Skinadre in a halter along the country roads where the famine-stricken people are dying daily. Even the saccharine intrusions of Mave Sullivan, who intervenes to save the worthless Darby, cannot quite succeed in spoiling the macabre ferocity of the scene:

> Skinadre's appearance and position were ludicrously and painfully helpless. His face was so pale and thin that it was difficult to see, even in those frightful times of sickness and famine, a countenance from which they were more significantly reflected. He was absolutely shrunk up with terror into half his size, his little, thin, corded neck appearing as if it were striving unsuccessfully to work its way down into his trunk, and his small ferret eyes looking about in every direction for someone to extricate him out of the deadly thrall in which he was held.

The minuteness of the detailed observation in this entire scene imparts an impressive power to the writing. There is a saving touch here of what John Montague calls 'the natural wild exuberance that erupts into *Valentine McClutchy* like a volcano', the quality of almost crazed brilliance which Carleton achieved more often in that earlier novel, notably with the unforgettable wise fool, Raymond na Hattha, who aroused Yeats's particular enthusiasm. Yeats sensed a distinctively dark mood in *The Black Prophet*:

> From the first to the last it is full of a mournful fervour strange to those who know Carleton merely as a humorist; and through all its mournfulness there runs a kind of unhuman fatalism that makes one think of barren moors at moonlight and leaden sunsets over sea. He has never used the dialect to such purpose elsewhere. It serves him for everything, from grotesque humour to intense lyricism.

One wishes, however, that Carleton could have sustained some of the more intense moods of the novel with greater tonal consistency. He shows himself capable of lapsing distressingly into unexpected bathos. One such moment occurs during the elaborate set-piece scene in Chapter XXIX where, without much regard to the exigencies of plot, Carleton introduces the parish priest, Fr Hanratty, and the Prophet's wife, Nelly M'Gowan, into a wretched cabin in which a mother and her three children lie dying in dreadful squalor. The scene, fictionally pointless though it is, is nevertheless a harrowing one, but Carleton brings the whole thing tumbling into absurdity with one ludicrous adjective from Fr Hanratty. When the mother and two of the children have expired before his eyes, he turns his attention to the little boy, who shows some signs of life:

> The priest, seeing that she was dead, offered up a short but earnest prayer for the repose of her soul, after which he turned his attention to the boy.
>
> "The question now is," he observed to his companion, "can we save this poor but interesting child?"

This kind of slump into the idiom of *East Lynne,* one feels, almost justifies the severe strictures passed on Carleton's use of language by Frank O'Connor in *The Backward Look*:

> Carleton is the very opposite of Griffin. His English is leaden, his judgement is dull, and he simply has no ear for speech. For Carleton there are not as many languages as there are people. There are only two languages—correct English and peasant English. Peasant English is further subdivided into honest peasant English and Babu—'sesquipedalian and stilted nonsense', as he describes it himself in a rare flash of style ... . Because of this deafness to living speech Carleton found it difficult to keep on one plane even for a page or two.

The Black Prophet, as it happens, provides but one welcome moment of characteristic 'sesquipedalian and stilted nonsense'. This is the pedlar's petition to Mr Travers on behalf of Cornelius Dalton, which opens with a flourish:

> "The humble petition of Cornelius Dalton, to his Honour, Mr John Robert Travers, Esq., on behalf of himself, his wife, and his afflicted family: now lying in a state of almost superhuman destitution—by Eugenius M'Grane, philomath and classical instructor in the learned languages of Latin, English, and the Hibernian Vernacular, with an inceptive initiation into the rudiments of Greek, as far as the Gospel of St John the Divine, attended with copious disquisitions on the relative merits of moral and physical philosophy, as contrasted with the pusillanimous lectures of that ignoramus of the first water, Phadrick M'Swagger, falsely calling himself philomath ... .

For a brief space, here, we listen to the high comedy of some of the *Traits and Stories* and confront once again the extraordinary mixture of modes and moods so characteristic of Carleton's work at all times. Anthony Cronin, who edited a selection from the *Traits and Stories* in 1962, remarked the swirling turbulence of the stories. His views on Carleton's ear for dialogue differ considerably from those of Frank O'Connor:

> What he re-created when he got into his stride was nothing less than the life of a whole people. It is a strange one, in its grotesqueness, its often savage humour, its perennial violence and its not infrequent horror. The world from which Carleton had come was balanced on the edge of extinction. Human life was little thought of, though the human emotions of passion, anger, revenge and loyalty were certainly esteemed. ... But though there is a dark side to Carleton, a part of him that seems often to

have been tortured almost beyond bearing by the perennial murderous ferocity of the human heart, beyond and perhaps above this is a delight in the re-creation of a world which to him, after all, was really the ordinary one. For Carleton is above all, I think, a great comic artist ... And his comic gift was matched ... by an ear for dialogue which, to mix the metaphor, never puts a foot wrong.

Carleton's extraordinary tonal fluctuations are matched, it would seem, only by the variety of divergent critical responses to him. In *The Black Prophet,* the grimness of the Famine background demands from a novelist who was at best an uneven performer in the *genre* a fable of unusual power to match the terrible facts of the world he is depicting. Carleton's failure to find such a fable is the more serious because of the great weight of horror inherent in his chosen scene. He conveys powerfully the atmosphere of the period: the incessant rain accompanied by warmth which produced rotting crops; the horror of the famine fever; the make-shift, lean-to sheds for the sick and dying by the road-side; the shallow graves which scarcely concealed the diseased corpses; the starving peasants grubbing for nettles and watercress by road and brook; the riots and attacks on provision carts heading for the ports with precious food incredibly intended for export. Yet, when he moves from the fact to the fiction, he can only fumble with sentimental heroines and hackneyed abductions and clumsy flashbacks to forgotten and tedious rural crimes. Timothy Webb, most recent editor of *The Black Prophet,* shares the general view that Carleton's best work is unquestionably to be found in the *Traits and Stories* but urges that, while *The Black Prophet* has its obvious shortcomings, 'the whole is indisputably greater than the sum of the parts'. Webb offers an explanation of Carleton's partial failure in terms of his concept of his audience and also remarks the inappropriateness of the nineteenth century novel form to his purposes:

> The reading public was composed of the middle and upper class citizens of Dublin and London and writing for them meant adopting a pose and a vocabulary which they would recognize and sanction. It also meant adopting the form of the Victorian novel whose validity Carleton did not feel ready to question. His predicament might be best described as that of a literary middleman, representing the peasants to their social superiors, sometimes exploiting them a little, himself sandwiched none too comfortably between two classes, to neither of which he completely belonged. Yet Irish peasant society could not receive its fullest, most adequate expression in the form of the novel which was created to serve the needs of the urban English reading public. Behind *The Black Prophet* there is a visionary intensity, a violence, what Yeats called a 'clay-cold melancholy', which chafes against the conventional framework of the story. Perhaps this power might have been better expressed in poetry, drama or even the short story, or perhaps it required a different kind of novel for which the English language could not provide a model.

Webb concludes, very reasonably, that 'though cramped and hindered by convention, Carleton has succeeded in creating a work of memorable and brooding intensity'.

Selected Bibliography

RELATED WORKS
Traits and Stories of the Irish Peasantry(1st Series, Dublin, 1830; 2nd Series, Dublin, 1833).
Fardorougha the Miser, Dublin, 1839.
The Emigrants of Ahadarra, London, 1848.
The Black Prophet was reprinted by Irish U.P. in 1973, ed. Timothy Webb, currently distributed through Irish Academic Press, Ltd, Dublin.

BIOGRAPHY
The Life of William Carleton, 2 vols, London, 1896. (Intro. by Mrs Cashel Hoey. Vol. 2, by D. J. O'Donoghue completes the 'life' from the point where the autobiography breaks off).
The Autobiography of William Carleton (Preface by Patrick Kavanagh), 'Fitzroy Edition', London, 1968.

CRITICAL STUDIES
Benedict Kiely, *Poor Scholar,* London, 1947.
Thomas Flanagan, *The Irish Novelists 1800-1850,* New York, 1959, pp. 225-330.
Margaret Chesnutt, *Studies in the Short Stories of William Carleton,* Göteborg, 1976.

CRITICAL ARTICLES
Patrick Joseph Murray, 'Traits of the Irish Peasantry', *The Edinburgh Review,* XCVI (Oct. 1852), 384-403.
Roger McHugh, 'William Carleton: A Portrait of the Artist as Propagandist', *Studies,* XXVII (1938), 47-62.
John Montague, 'Tribute to William Carleton', *The Bell,* XVIII (April 1952), 13-20.
Eileen Ibarra, 'William Carleton: An Introduction', *Eire-Ireland,* V, 1 (Spring 1970), 81-86.
Terence Brown, 'The Death of William Carleton, 1869', *Hermathena* CX (1970), 81-85.
Timothy Webb, *Introduction* to *The Black Prophet,* Irish University Press, Shannon, 1972.

V

Charles Kickham
KNOCKNAGOW

Charles Kickham 1828-1882

Kickham was born near Mullinahone, Co. Tipperary, the son of a draper, John Kickham. His mother, Anne O'Mahony, was a sister of John O'Mahony who played a prominent part in the insurrection of 1848 and founded the Fenian Brotherhood in America. The boy was educated at a local school and at home. At the age of thirteen, after a hunting trip, he sustained very severe injuries in an accident with a flask of gunpowder and, as a result, he became completely deaf. His eyesight was also seriously affected. For the rest of his life, he could communicate with others only by means of hearing aids, sign language and in writing. He could read only with some difficulty, holding the book very close to his eyes. In spite of this, such examples of his handwriting as exist appear to be reasonably legible. In his youth he was strongly under the influence of Davis, Duffy and the Young Ireland movement and was lastingly affected by the ideas promulgated in the movement's newspaper, *The Nation*. He became involved with William Smith O'Brien, John Blake Dillon and James Stephens, and played a leading part in founding a Confederate Club in Mullinahone. At the time of the abortive Rising of 1848 and the defeat at Ballingarry, Kickham went into hiding for a time, to escape arrest. Later, he became an active member of the Tenant Right League but seems gradually to have lost faith in constitutional agitation as a means for the righting of Ireland's problems. He wrote for a wide variety of nationalist papers, such as *The Celt, The Irishman* and *The Nation*. He became one of the principal contributors to *The Irish People*, the organ of the Fenian movement, and worked on it with O'Leary, Luby and O'Donovan Rossa.

He became a member of the Fenian organisation in 1860 and was a delegate to the Chicago Convention of 1863. In 1865, the government, well briefed by informers on Fenian affairs, swooped on the offices of *The Irish People*, suppressed the paper and arrested many of the prominent figures in the movement. Kickham escaped for a short while but was soon arrested, in company with Stephens. The trial took place in January of 1866 at Green Street courthouse, before the infamous Judge Keogh, and Kickham was sentenced to fourteen years imprisonment for treason felony. Confined first in Richmond Prison in Dublin, he was subsequently sent to Mountjoy Prison and from there to Pentonville. Then, on account of poor health, he was transferred to Woking Invalid Prison and was eventually released from there in March of 1869, having served a little over three years of his original sentence. Shortly after coming out of prison, Kickham was prevailed upon to stand for parliament in rather peculiar circumstances. Jeremiah O'Donovan Rossa, who was still in prison at this stage, was elected to parliament as member for Tipperary in 1869. His election was declared void and Kickham was then put forward in his place and came within four votes of winning the seat, being defeated only after a re-count. This was Kickham's last public political gesture but he continued to play an important part, with his friend,

John O'Leary, in the activities of the Irish Republican Brotherhood, behind the scenes. Together, they continued to promote the pure Fenian doctrine of opposition to parliamentary agitation in any form.

In 1879, Kickham went to Paris with other members of the I.R.B., for a meeting with Michael Davitt, to discuss the 'New Departure' policy which advocated support for parliamentary activists. This meeting went badly, partly because of Kickham's deafness, but the parties involved were, in any case, irreconcilable in their views. Davitt was to develop his policies through the Land League and Kickham continued to refuse to have anything to do with constitutional politics within a system which he saw as fundamentally corrupt. Irish politics were now to go the way of Davitt and Parnell. Kickham's failing health removed him from the centre of the stage. He retired to Blackrock, Co. Dublin, where he lived with friends until his death from a paralytic stroke in August, 1882. His body was taken in procession through the crowded streets of Dublin with considerable public honour and he was buried in his native place, Mullinahone. The impression of him which survives is of a gentle, idealistic figure, opposed to violence and filled with a deep love of his own Tipperary locality. When he was asked what he had missed while in prison, he answered memorably, 'Children, and women and fires'. He cherished a romantic notion of Ireland's struggle and was not prepared to promote his political views by violent guerilla tactics. Of all the Fenians, he appears to have been closest in spirit to the ideals of those earlier patriots of the Young Ireland movement. Although some of his contributions to *The Irish People* were of an anti-clerical tone, in that they attacked the Irish hierarchy's support for the *status-quo,* he nevertheless remained an ardent Catholic all his days. When John O'Leary's sister asked him whether he had prayed much in prison he produced yet another quotable reply by telling her that he had said in prison exactly the same prayers as when he was free. In addition to his prose fiction he wrote some of Ireland's best-loved ballads, among them such loved favourites as 'The Irish Peasant Girl' (i.e. 'She Lived Beside the Anner') and 'Rory of the Hills'.

KNOCKNAGOW

Benedict Kiely, most patiently sympathetic of commentators on the often flawed works of the Irish writers of the nineteenth century, issues an appropriate warning in regard to the works of Charles Joseph Kickham:

> Any consideration of Kickham as a writer must inevitably be influenced by his nobility as a man and by the fact, too, that he is a national piety.

Kickham the man lives in the Irish memory as the gentle revolutionary who, grievously injured as a child, nevertheless managed to educate himself into a passionate regard for the Irish nationalist tradition through the pages of the *Nation* and the teachings of Davis and Duffy. A prominent member of the ruinously incompetent Fenian Insurrectionary movement, he was to be apprehended long before the abortive Rising of 1867 and was to become one of the revered 'felons' of the land, enduring his prison hardships with a gallant dignity which won him respect even from his enemies and ensured him an enduring place in the affections of the Irish people.

His literary memory survives through his ballads and through one flawed but much-loved novel. *Knocknagow* is one of those botched but enduring works which serve as a useful warning to unduly pedantic critics of the form. Since it first appeared a century ago it has been constantly in demand and has been reissued in Dublin as recently as 1978. That it answered some sort of deeply felt need for a large body of readers is clear. It offered to Irish country people a sympathetic account of their ordinary rural doings, presented to them by a warmly enthusiastic Tipperary man, himself imbued with a deep love for his native Mullinahone. Ordinary Irish country people in particular took the book to their hearts and generations of country youngsters were brought up to be familiar with some of the book's most celebrated incidents and characters, with Mat the Thrasher's sledge-throwing contest against Captain French and the quaint sayings of 'Wattletoes'. Phrases from the work were adopted into the common speech of the people, so that someone who had never read the novel through could still tell a friend, as Mat the Thrasher told Billy Heffernan, 'the world is only a blue rag ... have yer squeeze of it'. To the present day, a Munster parent may still say of a naughty child that he is 'blue moulded for the want of a batin'. Kickham does for the Ireland of the third quarter of the century, the period after the Famine, what William Carleton did for an earlier period, but he does it without Carleton's irony and savagery. He described himself as being 'simply the faithful chronicler of the sayings and doings, joys and sorrows of Knocknagow'. W. B. Yeats, echoing this description, singled out Kickham's ballads for special commendation:

> Kickham's three novels, *Sally Cavanagh, Knocknagow* and *For the Old Land* are devoted to one subject—a conscientious, laborious study of Irish life and Irish ways ... . One feels through all he wrote that in him were much humour and character, describing power of a wholly Celtic

kind, but marred by imperfect training. His books are put together in a haphazard kind of way—without beginning, middle or end. His ballads are much more perfect than his stories.

In fact, Kickham's work was marred not only by imperfect training but by a fondness for particular models of a distinctly non-Celtic kind. In a letter to Ellen O'Leary, sister of the John O'Leary whom Yeats was later to idolise, Kickham confesses his admiration for certain aspects of the work of Charles Dickens:

> Dickens with his exaggeration is exactly what I would strive to be, the ideal at which I would aim, but could never hope to get within leagues of.

This fondness for 'exaggeration' of the Dickensian kind leads him to clutter his novel with such deliberately contrived grotesques as young Lory Hanly, the awkward son of Attorney Hanly, who is the possessor of an unexpectedly deep bass voice which frightens the ladies and is much given to energetic dancing involving amusing leg movements and gyrations. Mrs Nugent, the comically drunken cook who puts in an appearance during the wedding scene in Chapter XXX, is even equipped with a sort of Hibernian version of Dickensian dialogue:

> She moved with great dignity towards the door; but making a sudden and quite unexpected detour before she reached it, Mrs Nugent came plump up against Mr Henry Lowe, who mechanically caught her in his arms, as, yielding to the momentum, he staggered backwards.
>
> 'Hands off, young man, till you're better acquainted,' exclaimed the fat cook, in an offended tone. 'I'm no sich sort of indivigel,' she added, as she shook the young gentleman from her, to his utter confusion and dismay.

Nor did Kickham's fondness for Dickens stop short at his grotesques. He evidently also relished the more sentimental side of Dickens and, hence, we have in *Knocknagow* the completely unnecessary but much loved figure of Nora Lahy, the consumptive girl who is the Little Nell of Kickham's book and eventually provides the inevitable, touching, death-bed scene.

Our emphasis on the affection felt by masses of Irish people for the work of Kickham might lead one to assume that in him we have at last come upon an Irish novelist who was aiming his work mainly at an Irish audience, where his predecessors had equally obviously written with an English audience in mind. Yet Kickham, though he clearly wrote for his own people, is, in relation to the general strategy of his novel and its slant on Irish affairs, every bit as rigidly constrained as were Gerald Griffin or the Banims. His principal device in the novel is the importation into the village of Knocknagow of young Mr Henry Lowe, yet another English 'stranger in Ireland' who is used by Kickham to introduce us to the lives and customs of the locality in which he finds himself a visitor. He is English and Protestant and as ignorant of Ireland as Maria Edgeworth's Lord Colambre.

Kickham sets his novel in motion by installing Henry Lowe as the house guest of Maurice Kearney, a prosperous farmer and principal tenant of Mr Lowe's uncle, Sir Garret Butler. Henry Lowe's mother has warned him of the hazardous nature of life in troubled Ireland so that he is, to begin with, prepared to be suitably apprehensive, as befits an English visitor to the sister island. Kickham then sets about introducing this English visitor (and the reader) to the realities of Irish rural life, managing to convince him that his mother's fears are groundless, involving him in a series of rural vignettes and also in a conventional series of love devices of an exquisitely tedious nature. This creaky framework of coy amours is hardly worth dwelling on for more than a moment. Kickham manages it clumsily, having recourse late in the novel to an unexpected and unconvincing flashback to an earlier love relationship between Mary Kearney and a student priest, Arthur O'Connor. This episode is dragged in quite late, to explain Mary Kearney's uninteresting despondency. For the rest, such entirely conventional figures as Grace Kiely, young Dr Richard Kearney and Kathleen Hanly are inserted into the book as mere props, lay figures in the respectable dwellings of Knocknagow, who gather in various houses to sing sentimental Irish airs at each other or initiate tedious conversations on various amorous entanglements. It is quite impossible for the reader to feel any interest whatever in any of them and Kickham fails to inject even a spark of life into these figures or any kind of genuine excitement into the structure of incident in which he clumsily involves them. The novel comes to life only when it engages with the local people of the village of Knocknagow, who are either poor tradesmen, or labourers, or poverty-stricken small-holders on the verge of starvation.

As a visitor, Mr Henry Lowe is introduced to a number of Irish customs and practices, all of which are described in great detail. Important among these is his visit to a Catholic church soon after his arrival. In company with the Kearneys, he attends early morning Mass in the role of interested but uncomprehending spectator. The scene bears comparison with the visit paid by the Bartons to a Mass in George Moore's *A Drama in Muslin*. In that novel, the Bartons, though they are Catholics, are made to find the frieze-clad peasant congregation grossly offensive and oppressive to their fastidious senses, and Moore's emphasis is on the squalor of the surroundings, the raucous coughing and phlegm-hawking of the worshippers. Kickham, on the other hand, offers us a Protestant onlooker who finds himself, though alien to it all, nevertheless profoundly impressed by the deep piety of the congregation and immensely interested by the highly rhetorical sermon delivered by the officiating priest:

> ... in spite of his prejudices, the ceremony and the evidently earnest devotion of the worshippers impressed Mr Lowe with a respect for their form of religion which he never had felt before ... .
>
> A peculiar ring in the preacher's sweetly-modulated tones at once attracted the stranger's attention ... as he warmed with his subject he

moved about, now to the right, now to the left, and sometimes straight forward to the verge of the altar-step, which formed the platform upon which he stood—pouring forth what seemed to the unaccustomed ears of Mr Lowe a torrent of barbaric eloquence, which rose into a kind of gorgeous sublimity, or melted into pathos, sometimes homely, sometimes fancifully poetical.

Mr Lowe's initiation into the religious practices of the Irish is continued in Chapter VI where he watches the country custom of the 'Stations' taking place, with the three local priests, Frs Hannigan, M'Mahon and O'Neill, coming to the Kearneys' house to hear the confessions of the congregation, say Mass in the house, administer Communion and then stay on to breakfast with the people and engage in conversation on matters of general parochial and political interest. This occasion is entertainingly presented by Kickham who cannot quite resist introducing a certain amount of knock-about rustic humour, as the assertive Mrs Slattery endeavours to clamber past other pentitents to get to confession before them and comes a cropper rather heavily as a result. Fr Hannigan, having picked her up and dusted her down, admonishes her suitably:

> 'And now go and say your prayers and take the world aisy like a Christian. Sure I'll be able to hear ye all before I go, and what more do ye want? There's a strange gentleman from England looking at ye; and what will he say of the Island of Saints when he goes back, if this is the way ye behave yourselves?'

One notices here, once again, the emphasis on the English onlooker and this is, in fact, pervasive in the early part of the novel, as Mr Lowe gradually feels his way and begins to find his footing in this strange, new country. The customs of the Irish Catholics in matters of domestic and religious practice are sometimes compared with the corresponding practices among English Protestants:

> Instead of summoning the servants to prayers in the parlour it is the general custom, among Irish Catholics of the middle class, for the master and mistress of the house with their children and guests—unless the latter should happen not to be Catholics—to 'say the Rosary' in the kitchen.

Later in the novel, when a considerable range of characters has been introduced to us, Mr Lowe's importance as a point of reference in the work tends to diminish somewhat but for quite a long time he is made to play the standard role of the English onlooker at the unfamiliar Irish scene. When Dr Richard Kearney takes the visitor for a walk through the village there is an opportunity to reflect on the inaccuracy of the accounts of Irish life given by some Irish writers in the past:

> Though most of the houses looked comfortless enough, and the place as a whole had the straggling appearance which he was accustomed to associate with an Irish village, there was none of that unredeemed squalor

and wretchedness which certain writers had led him to expect. With one
or two exceptions every house had at least two windows. Several had each
a small out-house, and the little cart or 'car', with a high creel in it,
indicated that the owner was the proprietor of a donkey.

Later on, Mr Lowe is introduced to some of the idiomatic oddities of local
speech, when young Tommy Lahy explains that he has baited his bird-trap
with 'a bit of a biled peuta ... an' a shillig-a-booka, and a few skhehoshies', and
Dr Richard Kearney interprets for the stranger:

> Richard explained that the 'biled pueta' meant a boiled potato, the shillig-
> a-booka a snail in its shell and the skhehoshies the scarlet hips of the wild
> briar.

As we have already seen, Kickham acknowledged a fondness for Dickens, but
his clearest literary debt is to his Irish predecessor, Gerald Griffin. A number
of his principal comic figures are directly traceable to the earlier novelist.
Kickham's Barney Broderick, or 'Wattletoes', for example, clearly derives
from Griffin's Lowry Looby in *The Collegians*. Both of these comic servitors
are supplied with comic dialogue and both display similar physical
characteristics. Lowry Looby has enormous flat feet, 'like a duck', and so has
Kickham's character, Wattletoes. Both men are made a combination of
physical absurdity and verbal agility, though Kickham's version of the breed
is closer to the Handy Andy figure of Samuel Lover and not by any means as
genuinely astute as Griffin's memorable zany.

At the other extreme, Kickham's Mat Donovan, or 'Mat the Thrasher',
undoubtedly recalls Griffin's Arcadian peasant figure of Myles of the Ponies.
Both men are meant to represent the very best in peasant life, combining great
physical strength with natural dignity, restraint and gentleness. Both are also
remarkable for their natural quickness of mind and phrase and Mat's opinion
on matters of general interest is invariably sought by his social superiors who
wish to hear him deliver the latest of his rustic *mots*. Strongly reminiscent of
Griffin's *Collegians* also is Kickham's concentration on the middle-class
Catholic family of the Kearneys. These are the equivalent in *Knocknagow* of
the Daly family in the earlier work and Kickham uses them, as Griffin had
used the Dalys, to establish a strong feeling of domestic respectability and
family unity at this level of his society. If we ignore the contrived and
melodramatic handling of the plot-line, we can allow that the good-natured
Mrs Kearney, with her amiable snobbishness about her Uncle Dan and her
pride in her elegant tea-service, is an effective enough creation.

It comes as a genuine shock later in the novel to find that the decent and
respectable Kearneys, who have acted as hospitable hosts to the landlord's
nephew, are just as vulnerable to the iniquitous land system as the poorest
small-holder in the area and that they can even be put out of their property by
the malign contrivances of the greedy agent, Beresford Pender. In this respect,
Knocknagow becomes a successful exposé of the ruinous uncertainty of the

Charles Kickham

lives of Irish tenant farmers on short leases or, in many cases, without leases of any kind. Even the well-to-do Attorney Hanly, who connives with the Penders to get possession of various small-holdings adjacent to his own property, is at the mercy of a short lease and must await the landlord's or the agent's pleasure in the matter, like the poorest of the tenants. However clumsily, Kickham's novel gradually gathers considerable force as we see the various inhabitants of Knocknagow, from the impoverished Mick Brien to the well-to-do Kearneys, brought to misery by the inexcusably antiquated system of land-tenure under which they are forced to exist. Occasionally the writing deteriorates into mere sentimental elegy for the abandoned 'homes of Tipperary' but, quite often, when fired by this theme, Kickham writes with considerable force. One recalls, for example, the pathetic Tom Hogan who has slaved all his life to turn his little farm into a model holding, constantly draining and improving the land until his property becomes notable for its efficiency and delightful appearance. So intent is he on improving his holding that he cannot bring himself to provide a dowry for his daughter, Nancy, and she has to watch her pusillanimous suitor, Ned Brophy, turn his attentions to another woman who happens to have 'a saucepan full of gold pieces'. When he sees his poorer neighbours being evicted from their small-holdings, Hogan tries desperately to reassure himself that he will not suffer a like fate. He manages to convince himself that the raising of his rent is a good sign rather than an ill omen since, he argues, no landlord would be likely to raise the rent of a tenant whom he intended to evict. Hogan's frantic efforts to reassure himself of the truth of this argument in conversation with his neighbours become comically pathetic and when the moment of his final eviction from his beloved farm arrives he cannot bear the shock of it and collapses into delirium, dying soon afterwards.

It soon becomes clear, in fact, that Kickham's main concern in the novel is to depict the destruction of a rural community. One might have expected that Kickham, a prominent member of the I.R.B., a principal contributor to *The Irish People,* a man who had relinquished his belief in legal agitation and adopted an intransigent creed of total opposition to the established society of his day, would, when he came to attack that system in a long novel, have been likely to advance political views of an extreme nature. Far from doing so, however, Kickham employs in *Knocknagow* a poignantly elegiac tone and altogether eschews the more obvious kinds of political rant. It is in this respect that he approaches nearest to Griffin and it is indeed intriguing to see the cautious Limerick novelist, with his horror of the 'night-walking' activities of agrarian terrorists, and the Tipperary Fenian who had suffered in English gaols, espousing the same moderate solutions in their fictions. Both men understood very well the forces which drove the men of no property to desperate deeds but both also strove to convey in their stories a conviction of the peaceable nature of the great mass of the Irish people and a genuine horror of violence as a solution to social problems.

108

In Kickham's novel, the character who comes closest to violent action is the starving and desperate Mick Brien who, having been evicted from his farm, has had to house his ailing wife and children in a wretched lean-to which barely keeps out the rain. In Chapter XLIX we encounter Mick Brien abroad in the night with gun in hand, apparently bent on enacting vegeance on his oppressors, though his exact intentions are never clarified. Frightened suddenly by the appearance of an ominous bird overhead, he drops his gun into a deep bog-hole and soon comes to feel that his accident has been providential:

> With an exclamation of scorn at being frightened like a child, he stooped to pick up his gun. But he had been lying near the brink of a square bog-hole filled with water, and the gun had fallen into it, and, of course, sunk to the bottom. He knew the hole was eight or ten feet deep, and that to attempt recovering the gun would be useless. He ground his teeth with rage; but after gazing round the silent moor, and up at the peaceful moon, it occurred to him that the weapon had been snatched, as it were, by the hand of Providence, from his grasp; and the thirst for vengeance ceased to burn within him, and he felt as if God had not abandoned him.

Shortly after this, Kickham is careful to expound the moral for us quite explicitly and in entirely personal terms, referring directly to his own experience of imprisonment as his special warrant in such matters:

> No work has ever escaped our pen intended to justify such a deed as that contemplated by this poor maddened victim of tyranny. Yet when we think of his blameless life of patient toil; of his cheerful unquestioning surrender of the greater part of the fruits of that toil to the irresponsible taskmaster to whose tender mercies the rulers of the land had handed him over body and soul; of the pittance which he was content to retain for himself; of his terror and anguish on discovering that a felon hand was determined to tear even that pittance from him, and fling the wife of his bosom, and the little ones that were the light of his eyes, homeless outcasts upon the world; of the roofless cabin, the cold, the fever, the hunger—when we think of all this, we find it hard to brand Mick Brien as a MURDERER. And surely no one will for a moment class him with the human wild beasts with whom the writer of these pages was doomed to herd for years, and among whom at this hour Irishmen, whose only crime is the crime of loving their country, are wearing away their lives in the Convict Prisons of England?

His pacific viewpoint is not always presented to us as tediously as this. More often, it emerges in lively conversations at weddings or at dances and Kickham frequently employs his priest figures as spokesmen of a variety of political viewpoints. Fr Hannigan's sermon, in Chapter XI, is at once comical and painfully revealing:

> 'Every one ... must steal turf such weather as this that hasn't it of their own. But sure if ye didn't know it was wrong, ye wouldn't be telling it to the priest. And ye think it would be more disgraceful to beg than to steal

it. That's a great mistake. No dacent man would refuse a neighbour a hamper of turf such weather as this. And a poor man is not a beggar for asking a hamper of turf such weather as this when he can't get a day's work, and the Easter water bottles bursting. Ye may laugh; but Judy Manogue stopped me on the road yesterday to know what she ought to do. Her bottle of Easter water that she had under her bed was in a lump of ice, and the bottle—a big, black bottle that often gave some of ye a headache ... was split in two with the fair dint of the frost—under the poor woman's bed.'

The Fenian Kickham, to whom the Protestant Luby had left the writing of the more anti-clerical articles in *The Irish People,* must have had his tongue pretty firmly in his cheek while writing passages of that sort. Although he nowhere advocates violence, he everywhere exposes its causes.

In its own way, the novel is almost as passionately concerned with rank as *The Real Charlotte,* though it conducts its enquiries further down the social scale. Poor Tom Hogan is too proud to let his daughter marry a mere tradesman, but he has to die in that tradesman's house at the end. Even full professional status does not qualify one as a gentleman, as a conversation between Mary Kearney and her friend, Grace Kiely, indicates:

'Did you never hear tell what Sally Egan said to Mrs French?'

'No, I don't remember; but I recollect Sally Egan very well. It was she nursed me.'

'Well, your papa gave her an excellent character when she was leaving you, and Mrs French asked her what place she was in before that. 'I was with a gentleman, ma'am,' she replied. 'And was not your last master a gentleman?' asked Mrs French. 'Oh, no, ma'am,' said Sally, 'he's only a doctor.'

Grace reddened with indignation, and pronounced Sally Egan's conduct an instance of the basest ingratitude.

'You mistake altogether,' said Mary. 'She did not mean to make little of the doctor at all.'

'If papa is not a gentleman,' exclaimed Grace, 'I don't know who is.'

'That's my way of thinking, too,' replied Mary; 'but you see it was not Sally Egan's. It is only what are called "estated men" are gentlemen in Ireland, and their wives and daughters are the only ladies.'

The sturdy Mat the Thrasher is only 'a labouring man' and must bear that demeaning fact in mind when he goes in search of a wife. Phil Lahy, the tailor, is an alcoholic figure of fun in his home town but becomes transformed into a well-dressed citizen of consequence when he moves to the more democratic world of New York. Yet, even in Kickham's Ireland, times were changing and old Isaac Pender is made to ruminate about this when he has caused Tom Hogan's death by evicting him:

'I'm sorry now I ever disturbed Tom Hogan. Cary the carpenter stopped me on the road when his funeral was passing, and said, before all the people, that the coffin was his work, but that my work was in the coffin. A farmer dare not talk to a gentleman in that way. But these tradesmen are very insolent. Phil Lahy the tailor never puts his hand to his hat for me. And look at that old Phil Morris. I never like to see his eye on me. 'Tis these fellows that destroy the country. Only for them the farmers would submit to anything.'

Mary Kearney writes to Grace Kiely to tell her about all that has been happening in Knocknagow during her absence and describes how Fr M'Mahon has been so overcome by the dire miseries of the people that he has openly denounced the government from the altar:

Last Sunday, when requesting the prayers of the congregation in the usual way for the repose of the souls of those who died during the week, the list was so long that poor Father M'Mahon stopped in the middle of it, exclaiming with a heart-piercing cry, 'O my poor people! My poor people!' and then turned round and prostrated himself at the foot of the altar convulsed with grief, and could not go on reading the list of deaths for a long time. Then he got into a rage and denounced the government as a 'Damnable government'. I was quite frightened at the excitement of the people.

Characteristically, Kickham, having created this scene and having indicated the possibility of violence inherent in it, carefully defuses the situation once again. He distracts attention from the anguished and angry Fr M'Mahon to the pathetic death of a woman in his congregation who collapses on hearing her husband's name unexpectedly included in the list of the dead.

Knocknagow is a memorable exposure of colonial misrule, encased in a tawdry context of Victorian melodrama. What we recall with pleasure from it is its evocation of a small rural community, the warm-hearted goodness of its people, their small, pleasant dealings with each other, and their country pastimes. We watch them 'hunting the wran'. We rejoice when Mat the Thrasher proves victorious in his sledge-throwing contest with Captain French. We absorb something of Kickham's own deep love for his native village and the country community in which he grew up. Bitterness is often close to the surface but is never allowed to become the prevailing mood. While the small-holders of Knocknagow are being evicted from their little farms by the police supported by English soldiers, their strong sons are away in distant lands, fighting England's wars. At the end of the story, Jemmy Hogan returns to the village, having lost a leg in battle, and can scarcely find a trace of the house in which he was born. Kickham's determination to provide the novel with a conventionally happy ending is at war with his profound conviction of the sheer hopelessness of the situation depicted in it. The ending is chaotic and incoherent to an embarrassing degree. The historian, Leon O'Broin, offers us an insight into the curious blend of revolutionary and sentimental idealist which he rightly discerns in Kickham:

Like so many of the early Fenians he had a rather simplistic view as to how political freedom was to be achieved. It was a matter of rising to the opportunity that would present itself when the ancient enemy was in serious difficulties. One such opportunity, he thought, was about to emerge in 1877 when England's involvement in the Russo-Turkish war appeared inevitable. He immediately issued a circular letter to the members of the I.R.B. urging them to be prepared. As to how they were to fight, he shared the romantic notion of confronting the enemy in the open with, as it were, flags flying and pipes piping. He disapproved of guerilla tactics.

He scotched a plan to kidnap the Prince of Wales that John McCafferty proposed, and there was palpably no place in his make-up for the plots O'Donovan Rossa was hatching for the destruction of English cities with dynamite and fire bombs. Such methods, he insisted, were immoral and unworthy of Irishmen. He laid it down that if Ireland was ever again to become a nation, righteous men would bring it about.

Benedict Kiely, also, has summed up the contradictions which are at the heart of Kickham's fiction:

> It was Kickham's natural bent to be the writer of rural and village idylls, and *Sally Cavanagh* and *Knocknagow* have in plenty those glowing pictures of a contented simple people, but his revolutionary training meant that he could not ... confine himself to the idyllic things, to simple observation of the habits and ways of the people when they were left at peace.
>
> The harsh realities kept breaking through: of poverty, rack-renting, the emigrant ships ... .
>
> Kickham could become as melodramatic as any writer of tracts about the fate in store for Irish girls in the hovels of London or Chicago, but then in all truth the facts were melodramatic enough, and Kickham's ideal was a high chivalrous and remote one, a little too high for the world he lived in and very nearly incomprehensible in ours.
>
> Yet it will always be a wonder to me how a man with his physical disabilities saw and heard his people so well, unless it was that he saw and heard with his heart, that his very handicap increased his attentiveness and attachment.

His sprawling, clumsy, deeply flawed novel, riddled with sentiment and awkwardly constructed, earned its place in Irish hearts by means of the author's gentle, exact recounting of forgotten country ways and the patient sufferings of an abused peasantry. Though it is as gauche as 'Wattletoes' himself, its heart, like his, is in the right place.

Selected Bibliography

RELATED WORKS
Sally Cavanagh, Dublin, 1869.
For the Old Land, Dublin, 1886.
Knocknagow was reissued in 1978 by Gill and Macmillan in the Sackville
Library series.

BIOGRAPHY
Richard J. Kelly, *C. J. Kickham, Patriot and Poet: A Memoir,* Dublin, 1914.
James J. Healy, *Life and Times of Charles J. Kickham,* Dublin, 1915.

CRITICAL STUDIES
James Maher (Ed.), *The Valley Near Slievenamon: A Kickham Anthology,*
Kilkenny, 1941.
R. V. Comerford, *Charles J. Kickham (1828-1882): A Study in Irish
Nationalism and Literature,* Dublin, 1979.

CRITICAL ARTICLES
Rev. Matthew Russell, S.J., 'Charles Kickham: A Sketch with some Letters',
Irish Monthly (1887), 483-98.
William Murphy, 'Charles Joseph Kickham: Patriot, Novelist and Poet',
Dublin, 1903. (Facsimile edition, Carraig Chapbook 4, Blackrock, 1976).
Benedict Kiely, *Introduction* to *Sing a Song of Kickham,* ed. James Maher,
Dublin, 1965.
E. R. R. Green, 'Charles Joseph Kickham and John O'Leary', in *The Fenian
Movement* (Thomas Davis Lectures), ed. T. W. Moody, Cork, 1968.
Leon O'Broin, 'A Charles Kickham Correspondence', *Studies* (Autumn
1974), 251-58.

VI

George Moore
A DRAMA IN MUSLIN

George Moore 1852~1933

George Augustus Moore was born at Moore Hall, Co. Sligo, the eldest son of George Henry Moore and Mary Blake. His father, the benevolent landlord of a large and heavily encumbered estate, was M.P. for Mayo and had a passion for racehorses, an enthusiasm which he passed on to his heir. The family, which claimed connection with Sir Thomas More, was originally Protestant but a Catholic strain was introduced by marriage during the early eighteenth century and the novelist's mother was of Catholic gentry stock. He himself was later to spend a good deal of time protesting his essential Protestantism, sometimes with mildly comical consequences. He was sent to school at Oscott, an English Catholic institution run entirely by priests, where he managed to resist most of the attempts which were made to educate him in the conventional manner. His first literary enthusiasm was for Mary Elizabeth Braddon's well-known novel, *Lady Audley's Secret,* which he read at the age of eleven. He became determinedly independent in his tastes at an early age, reading and studying only what he took a genuine fancy to himself. Shelley and Byron were among his early enthusiasms and he was keen on Dickens and George Eliot but not on Thackeray.

George Henry Moore moved the family to London in 1869. He had won a notable election victory in the previous year and wished to occupy himself with his parliamentary duties. His eldest son was more interested in horses than in politics and considered becoming a steeplechase jockey, a choice of career which failed to win family approval. His father initiated the future novelist's first artistic interest by introducing him to the painter, Jim Browne, a family connection of the Moores and the model, Hone suggests, for the absurd Arthur Barton in *A Drama in Muslin.* George attended classes at the School of Art in the South Kensington Museum and subsequently went to an army tutor. Then, in 1870, his father was called home to Ireland to sort out a dispute with his tenants at Ballintubber. He died suddenly soon after his arrival at Moore Hall and George became heir to over 12,000 acres, providing a nominal annual income of some £4,000. In fact, however, when all the charges on the estate had been met, the new heir could count on an income of about £500 a year. He had no wish to follow his father as a landowning politician but decided instead that he wished to become a painter. He was still under age, however, and his mother refused to allow him to go to Paris to study painting. For the next three years, therefore, he lived as a young man about town in London. In 1873, at the age of twenty-one, he went to Paris and spent a year studying painting and enjoying himself. He returned to London in 1874 but was back in Paris the following year, studying quite hard. He was soon forced to admit to himself that he had no real talent as a painter and he now embarked on the social round in Paris and began to pursue an Irish heiress, Mary de Ross Rose. He had hoped that a wealthy marriage would help to restore the fortunes of his Irish estate but his wooing of Miss Rose was unsuccessful.

About 1876, he began his first real literary activities. He became friendly with a writer named Bernard Lopez and suggested that they collaborate on a play about Martin Luther. He met Villiers de l'Isle-Adam, who introduced him to Mallarmé and Mallarmé in turn introduced him to the painter, Manet. Moore now began to frequent the Nouvelle Athenes cafe, the gathering place of the celebrated Impressionist painters, Manet, Degas, Monet, Pissarro, Renoir and Sisley. His first published work was a little book of poems, *Flowers of Passion* (1878). This had a *succès de scandale* and was withdrawn shortly afterwards by Moore on the advice of his friends. In the following year he met Zola who was to become his first great literary model. 'There had been Shelley, there had been Gautier,' says Joseph Hone, 'now for a third time he experienced "the pain and joy of an inward light", and Zola was accepted as the inspired teacher and guide.'

The troublesome financial realities of his Irish estate now began to intrude on his idyllic Parisian existence. His uncle, Joe Blake, refused to continue as his agent and Moore had to find someone to replace him. At this time he had his first contact with the activities of the Land League, experience which he was to put to use in his first Irish novel, in which Mr Barton has to treat with the delegates of the League about his rents. In 1881 Moore settled in London. His first novel, *A Modern Lover* (1884) earned the displeasure of the circulating libraries by its frankness and this was eventually to produce Moore's celebrated riposte against Mudie's, *Literature at Nurse or Circulating Morals* (1885). Moore continued to apply French Naturalistic method to descriptions of English life in his next novel, *A Mummer's Wife* (1885), for which he prepared himself by visiting various English manufacturing towns with a touring company of *Les Cloches de Corneville*. His third naturalistic novel (he said himself that three such were enough to tax the endurance of any writer), *A Drama in Muslin,* appeared in 1886 and, once again, he had done the necessary field-work by visiting Dublin, staying at the Shelbourne Hotel and attending the State Ball at Dublin Castle. He was gradually to move away from Zola's Naturalism and come under the influence of other writers, notably Edouard Dujardin who was later to prove of such importance to James Joyce.

During the next decade and a half Moore continued to live in England, producing upwards of half a dozen more novels, among them the work by which he is now principally remembered, *Esther Waters* (1894). His *Confessions of a Young Man,* his first elaborate fictionalising of his own life, had appeared in 1888. The first decade of the new century brought his celebrated period of residence in Dublin where his house in Ely Place became a focal point of the Irish Literary Revival. The disenchantment with the old Ireland so vividly conveyed in *A Drama in Muslin* gave way to an ardent enthusiasm for the new artistic movement fostered by Yeats, Russell, Hyde, Lady Gregory and Edward Martyn. At the same time, his hatred of the Boer War turned him against the England of the day and he was to spend in Ireland a decade which brought him into contact with the major Irish writers of the time and established Moore as one of the great characters of the Irish Literary Renaissance, a figure around whom a host of stories and anecdotes soon began to collect. His Irish period produced the celebrated collection of short stories, *The Untilled Field* (1903), the important novel, *The Lake* (1905) and culminated with the completion of the first volume of his celebrated trilogy, *Hail and Farewell.* He left Ireland early in 1911 and *Ave* was published later that year.

Moore now settled in the house at 121 Ebury Street which he was to occupy until his death in January 1933. In those twenty years he produced a vast quantity of new works, novels, short stories, plays, semi-fictional works of an autobiographical nature and many revisions of previous works. Abandoning his earlier masters for the Pater of *Marius the Epicurean,* he began to develop a limpid, melodic prose style of great beauty. The apparently ineducable boy who had become a young man about town and a failed painter had finally, by dint of incredibly hard work, turned himself into one of the great English stylists. In obedience to the dictum that 'art is correction and correction of form is virtue', he became an incessant reviser, his own severest and most practical critic. His astonishing versatility may well have denied him the appreciation which was his due but much critical attention has been paid to him in recent years and he seems now, at last, to be gaining the recognition appropriate to his extraordinary talents.

A DRAMA IN MUSLIN

To analyse you must have a subject; a religious or sensual passion is as necessary to the realistic novelist as a disease to the physician. The dissection of a healthy subject would not, as a rule, prove interesting, and if the right to probe and comment on humanity's frailties be granted, what becomes of the pretty schoolroom, with its piano tinkling away at the "Maiden's Prayer", and the water-colour drawings representing mill-wheels and Welsh castles?

This passage from *Literature at Nurse or Circulating Morals* (1885), George Moore's celebrated salvo against Mudie's circulating library, though written primarily as part of his defence of his first novel, *A Modern Lover* (1883), has an evident relevance to the two which followed it, *A Mummer's Wife* (1885) and *A Drama in Muslin* (1886). The view it presents of the novelist's art as a process of scientific dissection carried out in a laboratory, strikes the true note of the Zola-esque Naturalism which was Moore's first chosen literary mode, one of which he soon tired. Its assertion that 'humanity's frailties' are the novelist's proper concern accords also with his early regard for the author of *L'Assommoir* and *La Bête Humaine*. Even the very details of the passage quoted above bring immediately to mind the opening chapter of *A Drama in Muslin,* in which a 'pretty schoolroom' resounds to something akin to the "Maiden's Prayer" so scornfully cited here.

A Drama in Muslin, Moore's first novel, is a work of quite remarkable range, looking back as it does to the world of Maria Edgeworth's Rackrents and forward to the lonely and striving heroines of Virginia Woolf. Appropriately, perhaps, since its span is so ambitious, it is characterised also by a sense of excess in its means and its materials. It is a book so rich as to be almost indigestible, crammed full of major themes and, though it lacks a hero, luxuriating in the possession of no fewer than five heroines. Moore himself, looking back at it in 1915 when he published the revised version of the work under the new, abbreviated title of *Muslin,* reminisced a little nostalgically about the zest which he had displayed thirty years earlier:

An engaging young man rose out of the pages of his book, one that Walter Pater would admire (did admire), one that life, I added, seems to have affected through his senses violently, and who was (may we say therefore) a little over anxious to possess himself of a vocabulary which would suffer him to tell all he saw, heard, smelt and touched.

It is a work about a dying Ireland and about a restless peasantry. It is also a book which, in its way, is as intensely concerned with women and marriage as D. H. Lawrence's *Women in Love*. In Alice Barton, his principal heroine, Moore offers us an absorbing study of a figure whom he himself linked with the Nora of Ibsen's *A Doll's House,* a young woman who puts away the beliefs and prejudices of her class and period and moves out into deep, untried waters of rational scepticism and modern individualism.

Moore's five heroines are intended to represent five different responses to sexuality. At the two extremes are the crippled Lady Cecilia Cullen and the lusty May Gould. The former, condemned to sexual solitude by her deformity, turns all her frantically lesbian perfectionism on Alice Barton until Alice's very normality repels her. Her devotion to Alice is then turned into hysterical condemnation and Cecilia abandons her Protestantism to become a nun, thereby going to the opposite extreme from Alice who is shedding her belief in the Catholicism into which she has been born. May Gould, Junoesque and amorous, is the first of the group to lose her virginity. Fred Scully, that literary second-cousin of Somerville and Ross's Flurry Knox, gets her pregnant and quickly abandons her, but it doesn't take May very long to regain her looks and bounce right back into the saddle once more, the picture of healthy eroticism. Olive Barton, Alice's younger sister, is the prettiest of the five girls but she is also far and away the silliest. With a typical flick of his claws, Moore tells us that 'in the beautiful framework nothing was wanting but a mind' and Olive will function in the novel as a pawn to be moved about the marriage board by her scheming mother. Alice, the older sister, is the plain one of the family who is ruthlessly used by her mother as a foil to the lovely Olive. The fifth heroine, Violet Scully, is a slightly curious figure who appears to have had some special significance for Moore. It is she who will rob Olive of the Marquis of Kilcarney in the game of hunt-the-husband which Moore sets going so briskly in the second section of his novel. Violet has a strangely epicene quality which appeals to the Marquis more than does Olive's more striking beauty. She is thin but elegant and 'a rigidity of feature, and an almost complete want of bosom, gave her the appearance of a convalescent boy'. The older Moore who wrote the Preface to *Muslin* in 1915, seems more interested in Violet and in her later fate than almost any of his other women figures and he toys in that Preface with a curious scenario for Violet's later life as Marchioness of Kilcarney, assigning her a hypothetical lover as well as an adoring husband. In the novel's first version Violet triumphs quietly over her mother's humble origins as a shop-keeper and wins the greatest matrimonial prize of her first Dublin season.

The book's elaborate opening scene shows us the five girls enacting through Alice's trivial playlet on the theme of King Cophetua and the Beggar Maid, the roles which will be theirs throughout the novel. Alice, the future writer, hopes that her work will be taken seriously and that the girl-actors will present it in an appropriately decorous manner:

> She had wished to show how a man, in the trouble and bitterness of life, must yearn for the consoling sympathy of a woman, and how he may find the dove his heart is sighing for in the lowliest bracken; and, having found her and having recognised that she is the one, he should place her in his bosom, confident that her plumes are as fair and immaculate as those that glitter in the sunlight about the steps and terraces of the palace. Instead of this, she had seen a King who seemed to regard life as a sensual

gratification; and a beggar-maid who looked upon her lover, not timidly, as a new-born flower upon the sun, but as a clever huckstress at a customer who had bought her goods at her valuing.

It is May Gould, in particular, who thwarts Alice's intentions by the braggadocio way in which she plays the part of the King. May swaggers about the stage, showing her excellent legs and generally alarming the nuns by her brazen physical presence. She is already manifesting those traits in her character which will come to the fore in her disastrous *affaire* with Fred Scully. Violet has resigned the part of the Princess to the petulant Olive and is herself playing the part of the Beggar Maid. This, of course, points directly to the main matrimonial plot in the novel in which Violet marries the Marquis of Kilcarney and, in so doing, scores off the beautiful Olive. The deformed Cecilia hovers on the edge of the action, jealously watching over her beloved Alice, bitterly conscious of her loneliness in a world where her twisted body unfits her for the only permitted form of female activity, man-hunting:

> Her fancies were so abrupt and obscure that none could ever be certain what would please or offend her. In one thing only was she constant—she loved Alice. There was love in those wilful brown eyes—love that was wild and visionary, and perhaps scarcely sane. And the intensity of this affection had given rise to conjecturing. When other girls spoke of men and admirers, her lip curled: had it not been for her deformity she would have expressed her abhorrence. At home she was considered wayward, if not a little queer, and her wish, therefore, to remain at school met with no opposition.

The entire opening chapter is a deliberate and rather unsavoury combination of fragile, conventual innocence with grossly sexual implication, with Moore manipulating his clerical figures with characteristic impishness. The nuns are transformed into procuresses, as they become excited by the play:

> Then every eye was radiant, and every lust delighted in the spectacle; fingers twitched nervously at the folds of the serge habit and lace mantle. Even the hearts of the little children rejoiced in the materialisation of the idea, in the crudity of the living picture placed before them. In a vision each girl saw herself selected out of the multitude, crowned with orange-blossoms and led by a noble husband through the dim church, from an altar where the candles burnt like stars, to a life made of riches, adulation, amusement. Like warm vapour, one thought filled the entire hall. The expansive matrons, on whose bosoms had lain this white-frocked generation, leaned to the grey-headed fathers, worn with a life's toil, and sought to express the complete, the fathomless, content that had fallen upon them. It was a moment of delirium, even the nuns forgot themselves; and, their sex asserting itself through all their vows of celibacy, they gloried in having been, at least, the providers of the brides of men; and in imagination they assisted at the wedding of an entire epoch.

The elaborately presented scene, with its detailed account of little girls in white dresses and the presentation of prizes, directly anticipates the central set-piece of the novel, the presentation of the debutantes to the Lord Lieutenant at the official 'Drawing-room' at Dublin Castle. The Bishop, 'seated on his high throne, the back of which extended some feet above his head', while little girls bob curtseys before him, enacts here the part taken by the Lord Lieutenant in the later scene. On both occasions, elaborate and sterile social courtesies are lavishly enacted and both are undercut by the genuine human passions which run just below the surface. May Gould's earthy sexuality troubles the watching nuns so that the Reverend-Mother has to send hasty messages of reprimand backstage, telling her to behave in a more suitably refined manner. The Lord-Lieutenant's Drawing-room is nothing more than a huge marriage-mart, susurrating with malicious gossip, speculation and envy. In neither of these settings can Alice Barton feel anything but an alien and she is quickly made to recoil also from the religious mummery of her school as well as from its grosser social implications. She alone among the throng finds the stage representation of the Nativity scene intolerably false:

> The picture of the world's Redemption was depicted with such taste, that a murmur of pious admiration sighed throughout the hall ... . The humanity of the Bethlehem mystery held the world in the nineteenth, as it had done in the first century. To Alice alone did the representation appear absurd, grotesque; her clear mind forced her to deny God's presence in a drama, so obviously one of human invention. The stuffed ox and ass were irresistibly comic, but knowing that Cecilia's wistful brown eyes were fixed upon her, she bit her lips and avoided a smile.

Alice's reactions at this point prepare us for her rejection of belief later. Moore will deploy similar conjunctions of the sacred and the profane throughout. The arrangements for the outrageously vulgar Spinsters' Ball in Ballinasloe will be initiated in whispers during Mass, when the Bartons and the Goulds meet unexpectedly in the local chapel and, ignoring their sacred surroundings, gossip as excitedly as if they were in a tea-shop. The fundamental disarray of moral values is similarly captured in the second section of the book where Moore satirises the contradictions of Dublin society in a Pope-ean manner:

> We are in a land of echoes and shadows. Lying, mincing, grimacing—careless of all but the pleasures of scandal and marriage, trailing their ignorance, arrogantly the poor shades go by. Gossip and waltz tunes are all that they know. Is there a girl or young man in Dublin who has read a play of Shakespeare, a novel of Balzac, a poem of Shelley? Is there one who could say for certain that Leonardo da Vinci was neither comic-singer nor patriot?—No. Like children, the young and the old, run hither and thither, seeking in Liddell oblivion of the Land League. Catholic in name, they curse the Pope for not helping them in their affliction; moralists by

tradition, they accept at their parties women who parade their lovers to the town from the top of a tramcar. In Dublin there is baptism in tea and communion in a cutlet.

It is, of course, vital to the success of the work that Moore should effectively fuse his two main themes, the muslin mummery of the women and the exposure of the political sterility of Anglo-Ireland. *A Drama in Muslin,* as he makes abundantly clear throughout, is intended as an exposure of an entire society and of the system which underpins it:

> The history of a nation as often lies hidden in social wrongs and domestic griefs as in the story of revolution, and if it be for the historian to narrate the one, it is for the novelist to dissect and explain the other; and who would say which is of the most vital importance—the thunder of the people against the oppression of the Castle, or the unnatural sterility, the cruel idleness of mind and body of the muslin martyrs who cover with their white skirts the shames of Cork Hill?

Anglo-Ireland, in addition to being a heart-breaking trap for free spirits such as Alice Barton, is, in Moore's representation of it, a ruinously matriarchal society. Mrs Barton is at the centre of the stage, dominating and manipulating her remarkably silly husband who gradually develops into a figure of splendidly comic impotence. Mrs Barton also manipulates the elderly fop, Lord Dungory, pampering him with her lavish hospitality, pandering to his absurdly Frenchified vanity and constantly using him in her battles with his two puritanical daughters, Lady Sarah and Lady Jane. Dungory, plumply corseted into outdated fashions, mouthing silly compliments to anything in skirts and afraid to drive home to Dungory Castle late at night, becomes emblematic of the decadence of Anglo-Irish gentry life.

The other males who appear at the dinner-tables of Brookfield and Dungory Castle are equally unattractive in their various ways and we sympathise with Alice's disgusted rejection of them. Mr Adair who 'took honours at Trinity' is a minor character whose absurdity is sketched with Dickensian malice. Whenever he appears we are likely to be told that Mr Gladstone is expected shortly to send for him. Mr Gladstone, however, manages to struggle along without Mr Adair's assistance and, in the meantime, Mr Adair is free to destroy the conviviality of various dinner-tables with his gloomy and boring political pronouncements. Mr Lynch and his cousin, 'Pathre', otherwise Mr Ryan, are a pair of unwashed country bumpkins whose wealth alone entitles them to a seat at Lord Dungory's table. Alongside them, the handsome English Captain Hibbert, with whom Olive falls in love, seems a very paragon of virility but his contribution to the conversation, an account of the latest assassination of a landlord, is hardly calculated to brighten the company's mood. Lady Jane and Lady Sarah, a grim pair of Protestant proselytisers, preside at their father's board, keeping a watchful eye on Mrs Barton and doing their best to subvert her matrimonial schemes. They are held in check only by their dependence on their father and their awareness of Mrs Barton's influence over him in money matters.

Thus, at the gentry level of the story, we are quickly acquainted with the essential ingredients of the situation. Moore conveys forcefully Alice's chilling sense of spiritual and intellectual loneliness, which afflicts her just at the point in her development where she most needs the support of a kindred spirit. She turns quite naturally to her father but is soon forced to acknowledge, with a sort of contemptuous affection, that she cannot look to him for any real comfort. Arthur Barton sings Italian songs to the guitar, paints monstrously absurd canvases of gigantic ineptitude and depends on his domineering wife for the money which purchases his paints and other comforts. His room-full of enormous paintings of historical nudes, on some of whom he hilariously paints the heads of Olive and Mrs Barton, is made into a Rabelaisian reflection of the novel's central concerns. 'War and women were the two poles of Arthur's mind', we are told. These are also, of course, the two poles of the book itself, in the sense that Moore sees the Anglo-Ireland of his muslin martyrs as menaced by an enraged peasantry and the forces of the Land League. Even Arthur's ridiculous canvases are to the point. His favourite subjects such as 'Cain shielding his wife from wild beasts', or 'The Bridal of Triermain' or 'The Rape of the Sabines', reflect in their endless repetition the incessant muslin mummery of the society.

If she finds naught for her comfort at Brookfield, Alice can only be further depressed by the other houses in the neighbourhood. They contain such pathetic figures as the three Brennan sisters, Gladys, Zoe and Emily, ranging in age from thirty to thirty five, living out lives of utter futility, doomed to make the annual visit to the Shelbourne Hotel, buy their costly ball gowns, make the rounds of the dances and the tea-parties, gradually fading into the age where they must join the ranks of the superannuated chaperones. The Brennans, chilling forerunners of the three Langrishe sisters in Aidan Higgin's *Langrishe Go Down* (1966), pathetically chatter about the nuns at St Leonard's Convent whom they recall from their distant schooldays, and gossip about the marriage-market in which their own fading charms annually acquire a diminishing value. Moore succeeds in making us feel the poignancy of the situation of these women. We find ourselves calculating their ages and guessing their chances and, most of all, dreading their significance for the eventual fate of Alice Barton, whose lack of obvious beauty would seem to doom her to the spinsterish fate of such as the three Miss Brennans and the seven Honourable Miss Gores. It is at this moment also that Alice sheds her last shreds of belief in Christianity, so that she cannot even fall back on conventional pieties as an escape from her sense of dark isolation. Her dilemma is fearsome and we are spared none of its oppressive claustrophobia. Only Cecilia Cullen knows of Alice's agnosticism and to Cecilia Alice spells out her terror:

> "Alas! we know nothing; we are perhaps no more than a lot of flies struggling in a water-jug. It is a very cruel creed. The sense of annihilation

is a black, a heavy burden to bear, and no one will ever know what I have suffered. I am isolated from the rest of the world. At home I am like a stranger; I have not a thought in common with anyone."

As one would expect of the author of *Esther Waters,* Moore does not fall into the trap of sentimentalising his principal heroine. Alice is not made to seem in the least heroic. She makes no public stand for her principles, strikes no martyr-like poses. The failure of the Christians about her to live up to the full logic of the creed they profess, combined with her reading of Darwin and Shelley, gradually strips this supremely unselfish perfectionist of her inherited beliefs, but she will not outrage her family by missing Mass on Sunday. She has already begun 'to see something wrong in each big house being surrounded by a hundred smaller ones, all working to keep it in sloth and luxury' but she will go through the social motions required of her even though her nature recoils inwardly from the mummery about her. Only at the very end, when she leaves Ireland altogether with her husband, Dr Reed, will Alice finally break with the Anglo-Ireland which she has for long rejected in her heart.

In the first great farcical set-piece of the novel, Moore again fuses his two main themes. The Spinsters' Ball at Ballinasloe, which is in its first conception a desperate piece of late-nineteenth-century feminism, mockingly anticipates the other great ball scene at Dublin Castle. The muslin martyrs, the young gentry women of Ireland, are traditionally paraded at great, organised dances. It is at such functions that the current crop of maidens is put on display. What could be more deliciously appropriate, therefore, than a ball organised by the victims themselves? May Gould is an appropriate organiser-in-chief. She upsets her mother by the frankness with which she summarises the predicament of the young and youngish women of the locality, but Moore employs the vulgar Mrs Gould effectively to reveal the grossness of the matrimonial calculation which is constantly at work. She warns the rebellious May that a bad marriage is better than none, since 'it is far better to be minding your own children than your sister's or your brother's children' and she irritates May by defending the tedious Mr Adair whose various political pamphlets have already bored the lively May half to death.

The survey which May and Mrs Gould conduct, in Alice's presence, of the eligible males of the area proves a depressing experience. The drunken Sir Richard; the licentious Sir Charles, with his brood of peasant bastards; the dreary Adair; the bumpkins Lynch and Ryan; the scapegrace Fred Scully; they make an unattractive list. Yet the girls press on with their preparations for the ball in the school-house and it develops, in Moore's capable hands, into an exposé, at once diverting and alarming, of the fundamental chaos of Anglo-Ireland and the menace which threatens it from an outraged and abused peasantry. As the gentry of the West of Ireland cavort in the schoolroom, they are aware of the faces of the local people pressed against the window panes, looking in at the vulgar antics of their 'betters':

"But look!" said Alice, "look at all those poor people staring in at the window. Isn't it dreadful that they, in the dark and cold, should be watching us dancing in our beautiful dresses, and in our warm bright room?"

"You don't want to ask them in, do you?"

"Of course not, but it seems very sinister; does it not seem so to you?"

"I don't know what you mean by its being sinister; but sinister or not, it couldn't be helped; for if we had nailed up every window we should have simply died of heat."

As the various beauties parade and the chaperones assemble, the note of sexual tension and matrimonial rivalry is struck and the affair becomes a grotesque foretaste of the more formal and correct proceedings which take place under the auspices of the Lord Lieutenant later. Violet Scully arrives in white satin, looking like 'an Indian carved ivory'. The more striking Olive is paraded like a beautiful mare:

Already the first notes of the waltz had been shrieked out by the fiddle, and Mr Fred Scully, with May's red tresses on his shoulder, was about to start, when Mrs Barton and Olive entered. She was in white silk, so tightly drawn back that every line of her supple thighs, and every plumpness of the superb haunches was seen; and the double garland of geraniums that encircled the tulle veiling seemed like flowers of blood scattered on virgin snow.

In the course of the increasingly rowdy evening, the unobtrusive Mr Burke is suddenly transformed into a Marquis by the dreadful news of his brother's assassination and he cries out in ineffectual fury to the faces at the windows 'Oh! you brutes! you brutes! so you have shot my brother!' As the evening progresses and grows more disorderly, the Bartons, Lord Dungory and other respectable figures gradually withdraw and the squireens finish the evening carousing drunkenly with the maid-servants. The entire episode is both thematically and symbolically potent, vastly entertaining in its detail, directly effective in its advancement of the book's major concerns.

The revelation of Ascendancy crassness against a background of proletarian menace is to be repeated again and again throughout the novel. Later, when Mrs Barton decides to dismiss Olive's suitor, Captain Hibbert, Moore will juxtapose the encounter between these two with the simultaneous encounter which takes place outside on the lawn between Arthur Barton and his tenants, who are bent on achieving a reduction of their rents. The two confrontations serve to enrich one another. In one, a landlord struggles with his tenants and their Land League advisors to make the best of an increasingly bad bargain. In the other, the scheming Mrs Barton gives Captain Hibbert his marching orders as the first move in her matrimonial pursuit of the Marquis of Kilcarney. Both Mr Barton and his lady are fighting lost causes, as the novel will increasingly reveal. The dense and complex unity of *A Drama in Muslin* is nowhere more manifest than at this point where two apparently separate scenes are cleverly integrated without any sense of strain or any impairment of the realistic detail of either. As the chapter reaches its climax, Moore deftly alternates the two encounters almost line by line, binding together the strands previously separate so that the ineffectual Arthur and his petulant and scheming wife become a composite focus for the hopeless game they are both playing. What we are having dramatised for us here is an Anglo-Ireland beset by its two traditional opponents, the native Irish on the one hand, the native English on the other. Moore, divided between his allegiance to the Anglo-Irish gentry and his cosmopolitan leanings, torn between his Catholic and his Protestant forbears, in so many ways himself a living symbol of the ambivalent Anglo-Irish experience, memorably embodies the tensions of his class in a splendidly dramatic alternation of perspectives.

The dark background of menace and terror is never lost sight of by the people who posture and pirouette before us. No dinner-table is undisturbed by it , no ball's revelry unclouded by tragedy of one kind or another and Moore offers as prelude to Part Two of the novel a Dickensian epiphany of national terror:

> Gloom, gloom, January gloom, and yet no gloom to deaden the cries for vengeance for the assassination of landlords, of agents—for the cold-blooded torturings of bailiffs, caretakers, and other deadly deeds done in the darkness; no gloom to hide the informer, and the peasant cruelty that fell upon defenceless cattle; not gloom enough to stifle the lowing of the red-dripping mutilations that filled the humid darkness of the fields.
>
> The year was drawing to its close—a year of plenty, but bitter with the memory of years of famine. With hunger still in their eyes the peasants had risen out of their wet hovels; they seemed to be innumerable as ants; they filled the roadways at night, and on each Sunday, from the Land League platforms, their outcry for a higher life rattled, and rolled, and cracked, like thunder, until the very air trembled with retributive victory and doom.

Later, as the Barton women drive in their carriage to attend the Drawing-room at Dublin Castle on a wet and stormy night in February, Moore offers yet another confrontation between the Ireland of the privileged and the helots who make it possible:

> Never were poverty and wealth brought into plainer proximity. In the broad glare of the carriage lights the shape of every feature, even the colour of the eyes, every glance, every detail of dress, every stain of misery were revealed to the silken exquisites within the scented shadows of their broughams: and in like manner, the bloom on every aristocratic cheek, the glitter of every diamond, the richness of every plume were visible to the avid eyes of those who stood without in the wet and cold.

Alice, as she looks out into the night, thinks of 'the Galway ball, with the terrible faces looking in at the window'.

To equip himself thoroughly for the writing of Part Two of his novel, the Dublin section in which the Bartons, the Scullys and all the rest of the muslin martyrs throng to the capital to parade themselves at the annual marriage-market at the Castle, Moore went to Dublin early in 1884 to take part himself in the social activities which were to fill his new novel. Ironically, as Hone records, Moore's mother hoped that George himself would find a wife there. Indeed, Hone gives an account of Moore's interest in a Miss Maud Browne, an heiress whom he appears to have courted briefly, but this lady was to figure in Moore's novel as one of the most neglected of the muslin martyrs and was not destined to become his wife. He stayed at the Shelbourne Hotel, as so many of his characters in the novel do, worked on his current project, *A Mummer's Wife,* during the mornings and, later in the day, would attend various social functions. Hone quotes from a letter which Moore wrote at this time to Zola, indicating his concept of his literary role at this point in his development:

> I work very hard, and this time I hope to do a more solid piece of work. The success of my first novel (which has been noticed in the great reviews) has put me on my feet, and if I succeed, as I expect, in digging a dagger into the heart of the sentimental school, I shall have hopes of bringing about a change in the literature of my country—of being in fact Zola's offshoot in England.

A long letter to his mother on the 17 February, 1884, gives a detailed account of the various people he has met and the functions he has attended. He has been to a state ball at Dublin Castle and has found it 'very grand and imposing'. He has also been to a Calico Ball at the Rotunda and writes disgustedly:

> There was a Calico Ball at the Rotunda. Never did I see anything so low, so vile, so dirty. Dublin society has lost all sense of what is *la vie comme il faut.* Men blacking their faces to go and dance with ladies—it was awful. Marriage is of course the ruling topic of conversation ... .

In due course, all these experiences found their way into the new novel. The Calico Ball was used to spoil Olive Barton's chance of marrying Lord Kilcarney. When it becomes known that Mrs Barton and her daughters have attended this vulgar assembly, where they have danced with people who are socially unacceptable to the Castle, their names are struck off the lists of the private dances at the Castle and Olive's matrimonial chances are blighted. Moore went to Dublin again in the following year, 1885, and soon after his arrival wrote to the State Steward:

> I am actively engaged on a book, in the interests of which I came to Dublin last year to attend the Levee, the Drawing Rooms and the Castle Balls. I was not fortunate enough to receive an invitation for a State dinner party. Now, as my book deals with the social and political power of the Castle in Modern Ireland, I should be glad to attend the Levee in February, if I could make sure of being asked to one of the big dinner parties. My books, as you are probably aware, are extensively read; this particular one will attract a great deal of attention. It would therefore be well to render my picture as complete, as true, as vivid as possible.

Castle officials, however, manifested no eagerness to figure in Zola-esque fiction and Moore's application was refused. Always ready to enjoy this sort of publicity to the full, the mischievous Moore published his correspondence on the matter in the nationalist paper, *The Freeman's Journal,* and became for a time quite a hero with the leaders of the Irish Nationalists, who saw him as an ally in their battle against Ascendancy domination. Moore's account of the matter, as quoted by Hone, shows him in characteristically pugnacious mood, laying about him with a will and obviously enjoying the whole embarrassing business:

> ... it was as a man of letters, it was for the purpose of studying, not of amusing myself, that I applied for an invitation. Was that the reason I was refused? One would feel almost inclined to think so ... . The opinions I hold on the subject (of the Castle) will be found in my next novel, my writing table is covered with human documents—fragments of conversations overheard, notes on character, anecdotes of all kinds. I came to the Castle, not as a patriot nor as a place hunter, but as the passionless observer, who, unbiassed by political creed, comments impartially on the matter submitted to him for analysis.

The novel itself presents a forthright attack on the entire Vice-Regal establishment and on the elaborate pretensions of the Dublin upper-classes of the 1880's. In language reminiscent of Pope's *Dunciad,* the various officials and lordlings who throng about the Lord Lieutenant are likened to 'flies about a choice pile of excrement', and Moore does not confine himself to attacks on officialdom but goes on to depict a panorama of ruin and despair on a national scale:

> We are in a land of echoes and shadows. Smirking, pretending, grimacing, the poor shadows go by, waving a mock-English banner over a waxwork show: policemen and bailiffs in front, landlords and agents behind, time-servers, Castle hirelings, panderers and worse on the box; nodding the while their dollish cardboard heads, and distributing to an angry populace, on either side, much bran and brogue. Shadows, echoes, and nothing more. See the girls! How their London fashions sit upon them; how they strive to strut and lisp like those they saw last year in Hyde Park. See the young men—the Castle bureaucrats—how they splutter their recollections of English plays, English scenes, English noblemen. See the pot-hatted Gigmen of the Kildare Street Club! The green flags of the League are passing; the cries of a new Ireland awaken the dormant air; but the Gigmen foam at their windows and spit out mongrel curses on the land that refuses to call them Irishmen.

This scathing picture of the second-rate quality of Dublin life anticipates by at least thirty years the corrosive depiction of Ireland's capital provided by James Joyce in *Dubliners.* It would be idle, however, to pretend that Moore achieves the detached power of his great successor. Instead, we find that his intrusive political diatribes sort ill with the evident pleasure he takes in the day-to-day doings of his characters. The simple truth is that, in spite of all his political invective, Moore hugely enjoys taking us through the social whirl of the Dublin season and particularly relishes the pursuit of the timid Lord Kilcarney by Mrs Barton. While he hectors us about the inadequacies of Vice-Regal rule and the Anglo-Irish Ascendancy, he splendidly involves us in the tea-parties, the dances and the gossip, taking a kittenish pleasure himself in all the minutiae of clothes, jewellery, fans, visits, invitations, dinner-parties and engagements. His celebrated account of the visit paid by the Bartons to the dress-maker, Mrs Symonds, is a case in point here. Moore, who has displayed an absorbed interest in the details of the women's clothing throughout the novel, permits himself an extraordinary stylistic splurge in the passage in which he recounts the dress materials displayed to the Bartons and relates each to a musical instrument. As he indicates in his essay on Zola, *A Visit to Medan,* he appears to have had in mind here the passage in Zola's novel, *La Faute de l'abbe Mouret* (1875), in which Albine dies 'in a supreme hiccup of flowers'. Just as Zola had evoked 'an orchestra of scents' with each scent recalling the sound of a particular instrument, Moore trails the dress fabrics before us with each matched by an appropriate musical equivalent:

> Lengths of white silk clear as the notes of violins playing in a minor key; white poplin falling into folds statuesque as the bass of a fugue by Bach; yards of ruby velvet, rich as an air from Verdi played on the piano ... .

and so on, and so on ... . Hone also relates this extraordinary passage to Zola's *Au Bonheur des Dames* and to the symbolist Réné Ghil's theory about the correspondence between sounds and colours. At any rate, the passage so amused some of Moore's women friends that they invented a fanciful extension of it and presented their additional musical fabrics to Moore on his next visit to their home. Apparently, Moore mistook their comical additions for his own work and was highly amused when the ladies revealed their trick, not in the least resenting the elaborate leg-pull. The modern reader of *A Drama in Muslin,* when he comes to enquire the success of this famous passage in its context, may well conclude that it is a piece of outrageously inappropriate stylistic excess. Moore may have intended it to reflect the luxury and self-indulgence of the Irish gentry and may have amassed his fabric symphony as a shocking contrast to the wretched rags of the Irish poor whose miseries are made abundantly clear elsewhere in the work, particularly towards the end. If this was his intention, however, he hardly managed to achieve his purpose, since the entire passage topples over into farcical improbability. The elaborately contrived paragraph strikes us as a pretty unforgiveable piece of stylistic self-indulgence, grotesquely overdone and lush to the point of downright silliness.

Throughout this section of the novel, Moore's acute political intelligence is at war with his clear pleasure in the privileges of the class to which, after all, he himself belonged. His Gallic intellect sets him certain targets but his Anglo-Irish heart is still involved with the tribe whose decline he so purposefully records. A similar conflict of interests was to blur his next important fictional work on Ireland also, *The Untilled Field*. Just as *A Drama in Muslin* fails to resolve the conflict in Moore himself between his allegiance to the old Ireland and his awareness of its impending ruin, so also in the later work, although he seems to set out to satirise modern Ireland and its Gaelic past, he never quite drives the dagger home to the heart of his subject, seeming to be constantly seduced by the lonely beauty of the Irish landscape and the quiet gentleness of many of its people. In the final story of the volume, having inveighed throughout against the cultural philistinism of his 'unwashed country', Moore astonishingly and quite against the superficial logic of the work, has Harding decide to return to live in Ireland, in a climax which is the reverse of Stephen Dedalus's celebrated exit. It is also notable that when Alice Barton makes her break with Ireland and goes to live in London with her doctor husband, she is not released by Moore into any splendidly romantic destiny. She is despatched, instead, to an English suburbia which Moore describes almost as caustically as his dear, dirty Dublin. The move is from overblown Anglo-Irish decadence to British materialism and there is a curious sense of loss and diminution at the work's end which is hardly altogether appropriate to the central satirical purpose of Moore's novel. The closing pages take us on a tour of Ashbourne Crescent and offer us a glimpse of Dr and Mrs Reed in their home at No. 31. The 'honest materialism' of the area in which Dr Reed now treats his patients and Alice gets on with her writing, is meant to contrast with the indolence and unjustified luxury of Brookfield and Dungory Castle and the sordidness of the Dublin of 1882. Yet, Moore casts no very strong vote in favour of the new as against the old:

> To some this air of dull well-to-do-ness may seem as intolerable, as obscene in its way as the look of melancholy silliness which the Dubliners and their dirty city wear so unintermittently. One is the inevitable decay which must precede an outburst of national energy; the other is the smug optimism, that fund of materialism, on which a nation lives, and which in truth represents the bulwarks wherewith civilisation defends itself against those sempiternal storms which like atmospheric convulsions, by destroying, renew the tired life of man.

In the end, one is forced to the conclusion that *A Drama in Muslin* simply has too much to say and rather too many ways of saying it. This plum-cake of a book is stuffed full of rich themes and exotic styles so that it proves demanding for even the hardiest literary digestion. It abounds in the sort of splendid set-piece scenes in which Moore always took so much delight. The Spinsters' Ball; the great Drawing-room at the Castle; the magnificent ball scene in St Patrick's Hall, these, with their curious glitter and glamour live in our memories when we have long forgotten the political asides and insertions. Moore was to adopt a very different tactic in his next great Irish novel, *The Lake* (1905), in which he explores a single central theme of one man's self-realisation, by means of an elaborate orchestration of style and landscape. Fr

A Drama in Muslin

Gogarty, like Alice Barton, must learn how to escape from his setting, but our attention is never allowed to stray away from the tormented priest in quite the same way as it is distracted from the lonely heroine. The later novel is all concentration where the earlier is expansive and diffuse. Moore himself seems to have come to feel that *A Drama in Muslin* was a transitional novel. He calls it 'a link between two styles'. In the Preface to *Muslin*, he wonders amiably about the young man who had written the first version of the novel:

> ... but when did the author of the *Drama in Muslin* disappear from literature? His next book was *Confessions of a Young Man*. It was followed by *Spring Days*; he must have died in the last pages of that story, for we find no trace of him in *Esther Waters*! ... .
>
> He was writing at that time *A Mummer's Wife* in his bedroom at the Shelbourne Hotel, and I thought how different were the two visions, *A Mummer's Wife* and *A Drama in Muslin*, and how the choice of these two subjects revealed him to me. 'It was life that interested him rather than the envelope,' I said. 'He sought Alice Barton's heart as eagerly as Kate Ede's.'

That curious remark about 'life rather than the envelope' as his main concern in his first important Irish novel may show us the mature George Moore in the act of imputing to his earlier fiction concerns other than those of a pure Naturalism in the style of Zola. 'A soul searcher, if ever there was one' he dubs his earlier self, in the same Preface. Perhaps the explanation of the book's top-heaviness lies there. It is both an analysis of a society and an exploration of a soul. Both life and the envelope clamour for the author's attention and the result is a certain blurring of his focus, a doubt as to what ultimately constitutes his real target. Richard Cave, who writes perceptively about the novel's strange mixture of styles and themes, notes that the exclusion of certain ornate passages from the later version served only to impoverish the work, not to clarify it. He observes that 'in revising the novel as *Muslin* in 1915, Moore attempted to overcome this problem of style by heavily cutting all the lyrical passages, but the loss was greater than the gain'.

Top-heavy as it is, the novel has its own sort of adipose authority. As important a 'Big-House' novel as *The Real Charlotte* or *Castle Rackrent* it is yet not content merely to look backwards into the past, but attempts also to cast forward into the future, probing the identity of modern woman through the sturdy independence of Alice Barton. Moore, in many ways his own best critic, sums up for us the book's distinctive mixture of effects:

> A comedy novel, written with sprightliness and wit ... . A soul searcher, if ever there was one ... whose desire to write well is apparent on every page, a headlong, eager, uncertain style (a young hound yelping at every trace of scent), but if we look beneath the style we catch sight of the young man's true self, a real interest in religious questions and a hatred as lively as Ibsen's of the social conventions that drive women into the marriage market.

133

Selected Bibliography

RELATED WORKS
A Mummer's Wife, London, 1885.
Confessions of a Young Man, London, 1888.
The Untilled Field, London, 1903.
The Lake, London, 1905.
Muslin, London, 1915.

BIOGRAPHY
John Freeman, *A Portrait of George Moore in a Study of his Work*, London, 1922.
Joseph Hone, *The Life of George Moore*, London, 1936.
Helmut E. Gerber, *George Moore in Transition: Letters to Fisher Unwin and Lena Milman*, Detroit, 1968.

CRITICAL STUDIES
Malcolm Brown, *George Moore: A Reconsideration*, Seattle, 1955.
Graham Owens (ed.), *George Moore's Mind and Art*, Edinburgh, 1968.
Richard Allen Cave, *A Study of the Novels of George Moore*, 'Irish Literary Studies 3', Gerrard's Cross, Bucks., 1978.

CRITICAL ARTICLES
Milton Chaikin, 'Balzac, Zola and George Moore's *A Drama in Muslin*', Revue de Litterature Comparée, xxix (1955), 540-42.
Phillip L. Marcus, 'George Moore's Dublin "Epiphanies" and Joyce', *James Joyce Quarterly*, 5, 2 (Winter 1968), 157-61.

VII

Somerville and Ross
THE REAL CHARLOTTE

Somerville and Ross
(Edith Somerville 1858-1949
Violet Martin 1862-1915)

It was, as it happens, in church that I saw her first; in our own church, in
Castle Townshend. That was on Sunday, January 17, 1886 ... it has
proved the hinge of my life, the place where my fate, and hers, turned
over, and new and unforeseen things began to happen to us.

This is how Edith Somerville, in her nostalgic work, *Irish Memories* (1917),
records the profound significance of her first meeting with her cousin, Violet
Martin. It was a meeting which was to result in a deep and enduring friendship
and was eventually to produce one of the most celebrated of modern literary
partnerships. Violet Martin adopted the pseudonym, 'Martin Ross', coupling
her surname with the name of the family seat in the West of Ireland, and the
two women achieved international fame as 'Somerville and Ross' with a
series of fine novels and particularly as the authors of the 'Irish R.M.' stories,
three volumes of which appeared between 1899 and 1915. The two were
second cousins, sharing a celebrated great-grandfather, Charles Kendal Bushe
(1767-1843) whose biography Edith was to write in later life. The Somervilles
and the Martins were long-established, Protestant, Anglo-Irish, Ascendancy
families, the former based in the far south-west of Ireland at Castle
Townshend and the latter in the west, in Co. Galway.

When they met, Edith was twenty seven and 'Martin' (as Edith always
called her) just twenty four. Edith had already been abroad, to study painting
at Düsseldorf and Paris, and tended always to think of herself as primarily a
painter. Both women had already published a few articles and sketches but it
was over a year after their first meeting that they began work on their first
novel, *An Irish Cousin*. They embarked on this in a whimsical, amateurish
mood, almost as they might have begun to devise plans for one of the fancy-
dress parties in which their family circle delighted. There was at this time a
vogue for light, popular novels of a thrilling and melodramatic kind which
were known as 'Shilling Shockers' and it was to the composition of such a
book that the two cousins at first applied themselves. As we shall see, a visit
which they paid to the house of an elderly relative during the composition of
their first novel was to alter their concept of their creative vocation and supply
them with an artistic ideal of a genuine kind which they were to pursue
throughout their lives. They were surprised and delighted when their first
book was accepted for publication and when their second novel, *Naboth's
Vineyard* (1891), received respectful reviews from the critics they began to take
themselves seriously and decided to embark on the writing of a full-length,
three-volume novel. To begin with, they named it *The Welsh Aunt* but it was
to be published eventually in 1894 under the title, *The Real Charlotte*. Its

composition was frequently interrupted by commissions which the partners undertook for various journals, by illness and by separation, and by the many calls made on both writers by the demands of their respective families.

The novel was well received by most of the journals and, had circumstances been different, the cousins might now have gone on to the composition of further novels of major significance. As it was, however, they were diverted into the writing of highly successful short stories. The huge success of their *Some Experiences of an Irish R.M.* in 1899 led to a demand for more stories of the same kind. Their literary agent, J. B. Pinker, constantly pressed them to turn out more of the comic stories which had made them a household name everywhere. They published two further sets of these, *Further Experiences of an Irish R.M.* in 1908 and *In Mr Knox's Country* in 1915, the year of Violet Martin's death. She died, of an inoperable brain tumour, in a Cork nursing-home and Edith, shattered by grief, believed she would never write again now that her beloved partner had left her. Gradually, however, she came to believe that she could communicate with Martin's spirit through spiritualistic séances and that Martin wished her to go on writing. She began, appropriately enough, by publishing in 1917 a reminiscential work, *Irish Memories,* as a loving tribute to her dead cousin. She was to go on to write five further novels and various other works in the course of the next thirty years. She always insisted that the renowned joint pseudonym of 'Somerville and Ross' should appear on all her work. She believed that the spirit of her dead partner was actively assisting her and, in any case, two of the late novels, *Mount Music* (1919) and *The Big House of Inver* (1925) had originally been planned by the partners together but had been put aside as they felt the works were attempting touchy and sensitive subjects such as inter-marriage between Catholic and Protestant at 'Big-House' level.

Edith lived to a great age and, having been born into the hey-day of Queen Victoria, survived into the new Ireland of Eamonn de Valera and his successors. The partners' work gradually won generous recognition from their fellow-writers and the academic world. Edith was awarded the degree of Doctor of Letters by Trinity College Dublin in 1932. Later in the same year, W. B. Yeats invited her to become a member of the Irish Academy of Letters and, nine years later, the Academy bestowed on her the Gregory Gold Medal, its most important literary award. She lived on at the family residence, Drishane House, until 1946 and then moved, with her younger sister Hildegarde, to a house in the main street of Castle Townshend which bore the euphoric title of 'Tally-Ho', the name which the cousins had bestowed on the residence of Charlotte Mullen all those years before, in *The Real Charlotte*. It was at 'Tally-Ho' that Edith died in 1949 at the great age of ninety one.

THE REAL CHARLOTTE

... it was the old house, dying even then, that touched our imaginations; full of memories of brave days past ... .

The sunset was red in the west when our horses were brought round to the door, and it was at this precise moment that into the Irish Cousin some thrill of genuineness was breathed. In the darkened facade of the long grey house, a window, just over the hall-door caught our attention. In it, for an instant, was a white face ... .

... We had been warned of certain subjects not to be approached, and knew enough of the history of that old house to realise what we had seen. An old stock, isolated from the world at large, wearing itself out in those excesses that are a protest of human nature against unnatural conditions, dies at last with its victims round its death-bed.

The shock of it was what we needed, and with it "the Shocker" started into life, or, if that is too much to say for it, its authors, at least, felt that conviction had come to them—the insincere ambition of the "Penny Dreadful" faded, realities asserted themselves, and the faked "thrills" that were to make our fortunes were repudiated for ever. Little as we may have achieved it, an ideal of Art rose then for us, far and faint as the half-moon, and often, like her, hidden in clouds, yet never quite lost or forgotten.

(*Irish Memories*, Chapter XI)

The important moment which Edith Somerville identifies here took place during a visit which she and Martin paid to an old kinswoman who lived in an old and lonely house by the sea some twelve or thirteen miles from the Somerville residence at Drishane House. The 'ideal of Art' to which the passage refers burst upon them during the writing of their first novel and was to form the backbone of all their best fiction. What had been suggested to them by this moment of social and historical 'epiphany' was that they should become the chroniclers of the social stresses which underlay the decay of such houses, the perceptive diagnosticians of the decline of their own tribe. The sudden insight granted them at this time injected a strain of social realism into what had been begun as a trivial melodrama and the partners began to feel their literary way towards a definition of their distinctive creative function. They were surprised and delighted beyond words when Bentleys accepted their first novel and paid them £25 with a promise of a further £25 on the sale of 500 copies.

Encouraged by this, they embarked on their second novel, *Naboth's Vineyard*, which appeared in 1891 and was received by the reviewers with a seriousness which surprised and gratified its authors. This second novel, treated by the critics as a serious comment on the politics of the day, had hardly been thought of in that light by the cousins and in a sense constitutes something of a wrong turning for them in their creative development. In it, they deal not with the gentry group they knew so well but with Irish village people whom they necessarily viewed from the outside. The novel has much structural strength and some fine descriptive passages but little real insight into either character or motivation and tends towards melodrama in its climaxes. Perhaps its real importance lay in the fact that the favourable and serious reactions of the reviewers encouraged the writers to take themselves seriously as novelists with the result that thay decided to attempt a major, full-length, three-volume novel. They had moved quickly from the genteel dabblings of the cultured amateur to the full status of genuine novelists engaged in the illumination of character and motive in vividly realised settings. The composition and revision of their third novel, which began life under the provisional title of *The Welsh Aunt* and eventually saw the light as *The Real Charlotte* was to occupy them for the next three years.

The writing of what was to prove to be their most enduring and important work of fiction was conducted sporadically, in the midst of a spate of other distracting activities and frequently interrupted by the separation of the collaborators. They were themselves much concerned at the many ways in which their involvement in family affairs and a multitude of varied activities got in the way of their serious writing but the slow gestation of the book may have had some advantages also in that it provided time for creative reflection and may have contributed to the book's moral complexity and the fullness of its social fabric. According to Edith's account in *Irish Memories, The Real Charlotte* 'was first born at Ross, in November 1889, and achieved as much life as there may be in a skeleton scenario'. At 'Drishane', the Somerville home in Castle Townshend, they made a beginning of the actual writing of the new novel, which they both referred to for the next few years as 'the W.A.' (i.e. *The Welsh Aunt*). Edith even turned the original title into a jocose verb and wrote about 'Welshaunting all the morning' on occasion. The work went slowly and by May of 1890 they had only begun the second chapter. In the summer of this year they undertook a tour of Connemara which they wrote up in the form of descriptive articles for *The Lady's Pictorial* so, for the moment, novel-writing had to give way to travel journalism. It was late October before they returned to the novel and this time they made some really solid progress, as Edith recalls:

> In the following November we did five more chapters, and established in our own minds the identity of the characters. Thenceforward those unattractive beings, Charlotte Mullen, Roddy Lambert, The Turkey-Hen, entered like the plague of frogs into our kneading-troughs, our wash-tubs, our bed-chambers. With them came Hawkins, Christopher, and others, but with less persistence. But of them all, and, I think, of all the company of more or less tangible shadows who have been fated to declare themselves by our pens, it is Francie Fitzpatrick who was our most constant companion, and she was the one of them all who "had the sway". We knew her best; we were fondest of her. Martin began by knowing her better than I did, but, even during the period when she sat on the shelf with her fellows, while Martin and I boiled the pot with short

stories and the like ... or wrote up tours, or frankly idled, Francie was
taking a hand in what we did, and her point of view was in our minds.

(*Irish Memories,* Chapter XX)

In February of 1891, Edith travelled to Ross, the Martin family home, and
work on the novel went ahead, though often slowly and with many
interruptions. In April of that year they made good progress and finished
what they described as 'Vol. 1 of the Welsh Aunt in 16 chapters'. Edith then
returned from Ross to Drishane and Martin joined her there at the end of
April. Work on the novel went ahead slowly once more, the cousins usually
working during the morning and giving their afternoons to golf or tennis or
some other form of amusement. That autumn they travelled to Bordeaux,
once again on behalf of *The Lady's Pictorial,* to do a tour of the vineyards and
to write up their impressions for the paper. Back in Castle Townshend once
more at the beginning of 1892, they began to draw their novel to a conclusion.
In April they calculated that they had only about 11000 words to write and
Edith felt confident enough to write to an American publisher about the
possibility of having the book published simultaneously in America and
London. They experienced particular difficulty in deciding the eventual fate
of the novel's heroine, Francie Fitzpatrick, but finally decided that she must
die:

> We felt her death very much. We had sat out on the cliffs, in heavenly
> May weather, with Poul Ghurrum, the Blue Hole, at our feet, and the
> great wall of Drishane Side rising sheer behind us, blazing with yellow
> furze blossom, just flecked here and there with the reticent silver of
> blackthorn. The time of the "Scoriveen" the Blackthorn winter, that last
> flick of the lash of the east wind, that comes so often early in May, was
> past. We and the dogs had achieved as much freedom from social and
> household offices as gave us the mornings, pure and wide, and
> unmolested. There is a place in the orchard at Drishane that is bound up
> with those final chapters, when we began to know that there could be but
> one fate for Francie. It felt like killing a wild bird that had trusted itself to you.
>
> We have often been reviled for that, as for many other incidents in
> "The Real Charlotte", but I still think we were right.

(*Irish Memories,* Chapter XX)

They brought the book to a conclusion in a characteristically informal
flurry, quite literally as they both departed from Castle Townshend for
different destinations. On 7 June they worked on what they called 'the most
agitating scenes of the W.A.'. They rose early the following day and, as they
travelled by train to Mallow, the junction where they were to separate (Martin
going on to Ross and Edith to London via Cork), they 'wrote feverishly and
succeeded in finishing off Francie'. It was thus, in a setting somewhat
reminiscent of one of their own 'R.M.' stories, that they finally completed the
novel we now know as *The Real Charlotte.* Back home in Ross, Martin got on
with the revisions and corrections and early in 1893 they sent off the final
version of the last chapter to Bentleys, the London publishers who had so

delighted them by accepting their first novel. This time, however, the news from London was not quite so pleasant, as Bentleys would offer only £100 for the book, an offer which the cousins indignantly refused. They next tried Smith and Elder and, in *Irish Memories,* Edith recounts their response:

> Smith and Elder curtly refused the Real C. They said their reader, Mr James Payn, was ill. Can his illness have been the result of reading Charlotte? Or was it anticipatory?

The matter was finally settled in June 1893 when they signed a contract to have the novel published by Ward and Downey who paid them £250 and half American rights. *The Real Charlotte* was published in May 1894 and was favourably reviewed by a number of journals, including the *Athenaeum, Pall Mall* and the *National Observer.* The reviewer in the *Westminster Gazette,* however, gave the book what Violet Martin described as 'a violent tearing on account of "disagreeableness"'. Edith noted that her mother 'likes the writing of *Charlotte* but hates all the characters'. The aspect of the novel which seems to have attracted most notice from the beginning, even from reviewers who wrote favourably about it, was its sombreness and a certain quality of harshness in the characterisation which disturbed many of the early readers. *The Real Charlotte* seemed to strike most of them as a dark and intimidating work. Edith notes this, but is in no doubt about the book's real value:

> On the whole, the point insisted on, to the exclusion of every other aspect of the book, was the "unpleasantness" of the characters. The pendulum has now swung the other way, and "pleasant" characters usually involve a charge of want of seriousness. Very humbly, and quite uncontroversially, I may say that Martin and I have not wavered from the opinion that "The Real Charlotte" was, and remains, the best of our books ... .
>
> (*Irish Memories,* Chapter XX)

From Edith, who was in general of a deliberately uncritical turn of mind and usually unwilling to pass judgement on her own work, this constitutes an exceptionally incisive view.

It was, perhaps, inevitable that early readers of a novel so firmly rooted in its particular society should have tended to search for the possible originals of many of the principal characters. Edith adverted to this also:

> Very often have we been accused of wresting to our vile purposes the friends and acquaintances among whom we have lived and moved and had our being. If I am to be believed in anything, I may be believed in this that I now say. Of all the people of whom we have written, three only have had any direct prototype in life. One was "Slipper", another was "Maria", both of whom are in "Some Experiences of an Irish R.M.", and the other was the Real Charlotte. Slipper's identity is negligible. So is Maria's. She who inspired Charlotte had left this world before we began to write books, and had left, unhappy woman, so few friends, if any, that in trying to embody some of her aspects in Charlotte Mullen, Martin and I felt we were breaking no law of courtesy or of honour.
>
> (*Irish Memories,* Chapter XX)

She amplifies this in another essay in the same volume, where she reveals that the character of Lady Dysart was largely based on her own mother:

> My mother was a person entirely original in her candour, and with a point of view quite untrammelled by convention. Martin and I have been careful to abstain from introducing portraiture or caricature into our books, but we have not denied that the character of "Lady Dysart" (in "The Real Charlotte") was largely inspired by my mother.
>
> She, as we said of Lady Dysart, said the things that other people were afraid to think.

> *(Irish Memories,* Chapter VI)

The Real Charlotte brings its principal setting, the village of Lismoyle, to such vivid and sustained life that it would be easy to plunge into the heart of the book and ignore the effectiveness of its opening scenes which are set in a drab suburb 'in the north side of Dublin'. The opening chapter, in its faithful reproduction of a particular type of urban dreariness, anticipates by some twenty years the grim realism of many of the stories in Joyce's *Dubliners*. The arid Sunday streets through which Francie Fitzpatrick makes her tomboyish way home after Sunday-school are the streets which will later be traversed by Joyce's shop-girls and clerks, by his Eveline and Mr Doran and Mr Duffy:

> An August Sunday afternoon in the north side of Dublin. Epitome of all that is hot, arid, and empty. Tall brick houses, browbeating each other in gloomy respectability across the white streets; broad pavements, promenaded mainly by the nomadic cat; stifling squares, wherein the infant of unfashionable parentage is taken for the daily baking that is its substitute for the breezes and the press of perambulators on the Bray Esplanade or the Kingston pier. Few towns are duller out of season than Dublin, but the dullness of its north side neither waxes nor wanes; it is immutable, unchangeable, fixed as the stars.

When we recall Edith's remark, quoted earlier, that during the early stage of the novel's genesis 'Francie was taking a hand in what we did and her point of view was in our minds' we begin to appreciate the significance for the novel of this opening scene in the hot and dusty streets of a distinctly lower-middle class Dublin. The chapter owes much to Violet Martin's memories of her early days in the city and the novel is engaging here with social reverberations which are to pulsate through the book as powerfully as they did in the often troubled life of the Martin family. In 1872, when Violet was only ten, her brother, Robert, found it impossible to continue to maintain the family home at Ross. Violet, with her mother and four sisters, went to live in Dublin while the Ross property was put in charge of an agent and the house itself let to a tenant. All of sixteen years later, when Violet Martin was twenty six, she and her mother returned to Ross and gallantly tried to turn back the tide of family history by reopening Ross and living there. The letters to Edith in which Martin describes the return often read exactly like scenes from a Somerville and Ross novel and the significance for Martin of her exile to Dublin as a child and young woman is made clear in Edith's account of her partner's Dublin experiences:

> It was not until Martin and I began to write "The Real Charlotte" that I understood how wide and varied a course of instruction was to be obtained in a Dublin Sunday school. Judging by a large collection of heavily-gilded books, quite unreadable (and quite unread), each of which celebrates proficiency in some branch of scriptural learning, Martin took all the available prizes. In addition to these trophies and the knowledge they implied, she learnt much of that middle sphere of human existence that has practically no normal points of contact with any other class, either above or below it.
>
> It was a rather risky experiment, as will, I think, be admitted by anyone who considers the manners and customs of the destable little boys and girls who squabble and giggle in the first chapter 'of "The Real Charlotte". There are not many children who could have come unscathed out of such a furnace ... yet, when that phase of her childhood had passed, "there wasn't a singe on her!"
>
> (*Irish Memories,* Chapter VIII)

Edith is here tactfully skirting the whole touchy business of the Martins' genteel poverty during their Dublin exile from Ross. It is clearly very important for her that she should stress how her beloved partner had preserved her essential refinement and gentility even under the strain of financial pressures. The point which is being clearly made is that Violet Martin *knew* people like Francie Fitzpatrick but did not, of course, become a Francie herself. She remained Miss Martin of Ross throughout and eventually returned to her proper milieu at Ross and Castle Townshend, where she put behind her the horrors of middle-class Dublin and was reabsorbed into the gentry round of hunting and tennis parties and Big-House visiting. Violet Martin's early personal experiences undoubtedly imparted a *frisson* of actuality to the social discriminations which are of such vital importance to the world of this novel. Nearly twenty years later, in a correspondence with the M.P., Stephen Gwynn, from which Edith quotes substantial extracts in *Irish Memories,* Violet Martin was to articulate forcefully her dislike of towns and her instinctive preference for the countryside where she and her kind had for so long maintained a comfortable social and political ascendancy:

> I am not fond of anything about towns; they are full of second-hand thinking; they know nothing of raw material and the natural philosophy of the country people. As to caste, it is in the towns that the *vulgar* idea of caste is created. The country people believe in it strongly; they cling to a belief in what it should stand for of truth and honour—and there the best classes touch the peasant closely, and understand each other.
>
> (*Irish Memories,* Chapter XXVII)

Once the central action of the novel is under way and we have been swiftly translated, with Francie, to Lismoyle, we shall not visit Dublin's dusty streets again but the memory of their sordid implications lingers in the background of the novel to provide an important perspective for us as we watch Francie pursuing her hazardous social course through various levels of Lismoyle society. Later, of course, when she has angered Charlotte by her *affaire* with Hawkins, she will be banished to the Fitzpatricks' horrible house in Bray to resume the sort of sleazy existence which is now more than ever distasteful to her after her brief experience of the elegance and comfort of the life at Bruff, a life she might have made her own if she had married Christopher Dysart.

After the important opening scene, we move immediately to our first confrontation with the central figure of the novel, the redoubtable Charlotte Mullen, whom we first meet in the role which will come to seem almost her characteristic one, that of menacing death-bed attendant. She will later preside grimly at Mrs Lambert's demise and will also torment the sick-bed of the dying Julia Duffy. Her selfish pragmatism is not abated even in the presence of death itself and her greedy and unremitting calculation contrasts strikingly with Francie's vulnerable insouciance in everything which has to do with her own worldly welfare. The candle-lit scene in the bedroom of the dying Mrs Mullen is permeated by the special menace which Charlotte carries with her throughout. She makes an ugly and dangerous figure as she is described for us for the first time:

> Miss Charlotte gave the fire a frugal poke, and lit a candle in the flame provided from the sulky coals. In doing so some ashes became embedded in the grease, and taking a hair-pin from the ponderous mass of brown hair that was piled on the back of her head, she began to scrape the candle clean. Probably at no moment of her forty years of life had Miss Charlotte Mullen looked more startingly plain than now, as she stood, her squat figure draped in a magenta flannel dressing-gown, and the candle light shining upon her face. The night of watching had left its traces upon even her opaque skin. The lines about her prominent mouth and chin were deeper than usual; her broad cheeks had a flabby pallor; only her eyes were bright and untired, and the thick yellow-white hand that manipulated the hair-pin was as deft as it was wont to be.

When her slatternly servant, Norry the Boat, arrives with the great cat, Susan (and we wonder why a huge tom-cat 'that looked like an enormous football' should be so named), and the monstrous animal comes to rest on the shoulder of Charlotte's magenta dressing-gown, the cat seems to assume the role of a familiar and there is a peculiar nastiness about the way in which Charlotte thrusts the gross beast onto the dying woman's bed, ignoring Mrs Mullen's pathetic attempts to plead for Francie with her last breath. When Mrs Mullen whispers to Norry that she is to 'give Miss Francie some jam for her tea tonight, but don't tell Miss Charlotte', we are given a painful insight into her awareness of Charlotte's antagonism to Francie and the dangers arising from that. Charlotte looms in the dingy, ill-lighted bedroom as a large, menacing bulk while the tiny, dying woman breathes her last knowing that she can be but a weak advocate for Francie's cause. The entire scene anticipates ominously the central struggle of the novel, between Charlotte and Francie, a struggle in which Francie scarcely knows she is engaged. The writers are also careful to touch in a revealing moment of anger on Charlotte's part, which suggests that she is the sort of person who might, in a crisis, give way to her deepest emotions. When Mrs Mullen refers to Francie as 'a good little thing' Charlotte reacts with furious resentment:

> Few people would think it worth their while to dispute the wandering futilities of an old dying woman, but even at this eleventh hour Charlotte could not brook the revolt of a slave.
> 'Good little thing!' she exclaimed, pushing the brandy bottle noisily in among a crowd of glasses and medicine bottles, 'a strapping big woman of nineteen! You didn't think her so good the time you had her here, and she put Susan's father and mother in the well!'

We are suddenly made aware of the depth of Charlotte's antagonism to Francie but Charlotte herself also appears more vulnerable now. Momentarily, she emerges not as the dangerously dominant figure she seemed earlier but as an angry and jealous woman twice the age of ther intended victim. Her lack of control here has important reverberations later in the novel. Altogether, this first brush with Charlotte offers us glimpses both of her strength and of her possible weakness. The public Charlotte appears here in full figure but there is a tantalising glimpse also of another side of her (of the 'real' Charlotte, perhaps?). We begin to savour the ambiguities of the novel's title.

When the two principal characters have been thus introduced to us, the book opens up into its first large general gathering, Lady Dysart's tennis party at Bruff, where we encounter the novel's other main participants and, in a scene rich in minute implications, experience the special quality of the society of Lismoyle. It is mid-June and this is 'the first of the two catholic and comprehensive entertainments that Lady Dysart's sense of her duty towards her neighbours yearly impelled her to give'. When Charlotte arrives, the 'difficult revelry' is at its height. Somerville and Ross take particular delight in the depiction of gatherings like this, combining a command of the large, general framework with a malicious delight in the particular encounter. Charlotte's first meeting with Lady Dysart is a case in point. It bristles with implications which enliven our awareness of both women and extend into further areas of meaning for the book as a whole. To begin with, Lady Dysart openly bemoans to Charlotte the presence of so many women at her party, characteristically failing to notice the tactlessness of this approach to another female guest. Charlotte is not at all disturbed by her reception—she 'understood that nothing personal was intended'. She knows that Lady Dysart is treating her as 'one of the inner circle'. She is not, however, aware of the further implications which the authors wish the attentive reader to grasp, significant details of a sexual nature which are here, as elsewhere in the novel, cleverly suggested rather than openly stated. Charlotte, in being made an exception to the general stricture on the women at the party, is being treated almost as a sort of honorary man, a role she will fill again later at yet another party. At Mrs Beattie's tea-party in Chapter XXVI, while the young people are dancing and making merry upstairs, Charlotte is in the dining-room 'partaking of a gentlemanly glass of Marsala with Mr Beattie, and other heads of families'. In Chapter XXXIX, one of her tenants in the dreadful Ferry Lane is made to address her in a letter as 'Honored Madman', a moment of meaningful comedy. While Charlotte is preening herself on the special status she believes she enjoys in Lady Dysart's eyes, she is being exposed to us as a sexual failure, almost indeed a sexual non-starter, a role she will fill again and again in the course of the action, particularly in her encounters with Lambert. On the heels of this opening we are treated to another exposure of Charlotte's distinctive insensitivity, this time in relation to speech and accent, matters of peculiar interest to Somerville and Ross:

> Charlotte had many tones of voice, according with the many facets of her character, and when she wished to be playful she affected a vigorous brogue, not perhaps being aware that her own accent scarcely admitted of being strengthened.
> This refinement of humour was probably wasted on Lady Dysart. She was an Englishwoman, and, as such, was constitutionally unable to discern perfectly the subtle grades of Irish vulgarity.

The essence of the matter, here, is that Charlotte's role-playing is revealed to us as totally irrelevant, though she herself is unaware of this. We watch her as she presents yet another of 'the many facets of her character' and we see her comic contrivance revealed as entirely wasted on her English listener. Charlotte mistakenly believes that she is in control of the situation. This exposure of her has important resonances in relation to her role in the novel as manipulator-in-chief. Francie, also, remains sublimely unaware of Charlotte's manipulative role and, as we watch the progress of the action, we are treated again and again to the sight of Charlotte Mullen apparently victorious in all her dealings yet utterly defeated in what matters most to the heart of 'the real Charlotte', her hungry desire for Lambert. The comic futility of Charlotte's vocal acrobatics for the benefit of the serenely indifferent Lady Dysart is an anticipation of the ultimate irrelevance of her other complicated manoeuverings throughout the novel.

The writers' new confidence in their abilities is exemplified in Charlotte's amusing story of how she trapped Tom Casey, 'the land-leaguing plumber', in her water-tank and forced him to sing 'God Save the Queen' as a condition of his release. Land-league politics had got a rather more heavy-handed treatment in *Naboth's Vineyard*, but Charlotte's hearty account of her comic victory over Casey has more than entertainment value. In all her dealings with the local people she will be shown as a domineering and dangerous figure whose own comparatively humble origins give her a special understanding of the villagers' mentality. She will later intimidate the tailor, Dinny Lyndon, by her knowledge of the Irish language when she speaks a phrase in that language to indicate that she is privy to his private mode of communication with his wife. Not that Charlotte is permitted to have things all her own way at Lady Dysart's tennis-party. She has a brief encounter with Lambert and assumes an almost wifely, proprietorial air as she claims to have cured him of baldness but, hard on the heels of this, she is subjected to the intensely irritating suggestion that Francie is her niece, when, in reality, she is her cousin. Lambert, 'with a patronage that he knew was provoking', insultingly asserts that this is a distinction without a difference since Charlotte is 'what they call her Welsh aunt, anyhow'. This crude reference to the disparity in age between the two women infuriates Charlotte. Even in this sunny public setting, her encounter with Roddy Lambert, like all her encounters with him, is heavy with sexual innuendo. He is a smart and youthful thirty-five and owes his crop of black hair to Charlotte's ministrations. Francie is barely twenty. Charlotte is over forty now and under no illusions about her unattractiveness. As she chats her way briskly about the lawn, we are made to savour both her menace and her peculiar vulnerability. Even the inoffensive Pamela Dysart is made to repeat the wounding suggestion of the aunt/niece relationship, further angering Charlotte who 'showed all her teeth in a forced smile' as she corrects the misunderstanding once again. Hawkins, who is to play so important a part later, appears from the tennis-court to share a jest with Lambert and Pamela at Charlotte's expense, thereby angering her even further, and the scene is climaxed by Charlotte's conversation with Christopher Dysart, during which she has yet again to endure further irritating hints of Lambert's special relationship with Francie.

The novel's solidly convincing realism is grounded in its devoted attention to the lively depiction of a carefully stratified community in a series of minutely rendered settings. Lismoyle society, from the Dysarts of Bruff at its apex to the sleazy residents of Ferry Lane at its lower depths, springs briskly to life. The middle ground is occupied by such local worthies as Mrs Baker, Mrs Beattie and poor Mrs Lambert, Roddy's 'turkey-hen' spouse. We meet the dying Julia Duffy as she tumbles down the social ladder into her grave and watch Charlotte Mullen as she claws her way laboriously upward by every means at her disposal. The officers of the local garrison are on hand to add a touch of military glamour at parties and picnics. The authors' delight in detailed representation manifests itself particularly in the many Lismoyle houses to which we are granted entry. The houses themselves effectively reflect their owners and thus become part of the work, acquiring a special dimension of moral and social significance in relation to their owners and to each other. Appropriately, since Charlotte will be at the heart of the book, her euphorically named residence, 'Tally-Ho Lodge', gets a good deal of attention. The account of it, in Chapter IV, is a memorable combination of the comic and the gruesome. Norry the Boat queens it in the grimy kitchen, attended by her own 'special kitchen-slut and co-religionist', Bid-Sal, and

Louisa, the 'Protestant orphan of unequalled sluggishness and stupidity'. She and the aged cockatoo wage constant war against Charlotte's legion of cats. The house is claustrophobically encased in choking greenery:

> Opposite the hall door the ground rose in a slight slope, thickly covered with evergreens, and topped by a lime tree, on whose lower limbs a flock of black turkeys had ranged themselves in sepulchral meditation. The house itself was half stifled with ivy, monthly roses, and virginian creeper; everywhere was the same unkempt profusion of green things, that sucked the sunshine into themselves, and left the air damp and shadowed.

Charlotte will eventually move from here to take up residence in Gurthnamuckla but before she does we are given a memorable glimpse of the poverty-stricken Julia Duffy as she clings to the last pitiful remnants of respectability and struggles desperately to gain a hearing from the crazed Sir Benjamin Dysart. Julia is the product of one of those 'mixed' marriages (in this case, between her Protestant father and his Catholic dairymaid) which, in the world of Somerville and Ross, invariably presage social ruin and decay. She is a desiccated version of the aged relative who had so inspired the cousins during the writing of their first novel and she proves no match for the ruthless Charlotte Mullen.

Bruff, the residence of Sir Benjamin and Lady Dysart, is the 'Big-House' of Lismoyle. Three miles outside the village, beautifully situated by the lakeside, it is a place of elegance and refinement. We will later view its spacious rooms through the awed eyes of Francie when she comes there for her brief and socially disastrous visit. The Dysarts themselves, however, are a strangely futile tribe. Sir Benjamin is an apoplectic invalid who spends his time being wheeled about in a bath-chair by his man-servant, James Canavan. At our first encounter with him we see him crazily poking with his walking-stick at the visiting Englishwoman, Evelyn Hope-Drummond, as she tries to pick one of the roses outside the drawing-room window. This scene becomes a tiny comic vignette of the entire Anglo-Irish situation. Evelyn is the languid creature imported by Lady Dysart as a possible bride for Christopher, who totally ignores her. These writers always reserve a special scorn for this type of visitor from the larger island. The male version of the species can be seen getting his come-uppance in the person of Leigh Kelway in the lively 'R.M.' story, *Lisheen Races, Second-Hand*. As Miss Hope-Drummond starts back out of reach of the crazy Sir Benjamin's threatening walking-stick, she is gallantly addressed by James Canavan, the man-servant, who gives her the freedom of the rose-bed as though it were his own property:

> A bath-chair, occupied by an old man in a tall hat, and pushed by a man also in a tall hat, had suddenly turned the corner of the house, and Miss Hope-Drummond drew back precipitately to avoid the uplifted walking-stick of Sir Benjamin Dysart.
> 'Oh, fie, for shame, Sir Benjamin!' exclaimed the man who had been addressed as James Canavan. 'Pray, cull the rose, miss,' he continued, with a flourish of his hand; 'sweets to the sweet!'

'Whom the gods wish to destroy they first make mad', and this brief encounter in the course of which the native Irish man-servant gallantly offers his Anglo-Irish master's roses to an English visitor is both funny and meaningful. It offers in embryo a tiny and witty version of the writers' preoccupation with the displacement of the Anglo-Irish Ascendancy landlords by the native Irish. Lady Dysart, thirty years her husband's junior, is meantime busily gardening with her daughter, Pamela. Very much the *grande-dame* of Lismoyle, she is here given a memorably reductive treatment, as she is shown to have planted an entire flower-bed with chickweed plants which she has mistaken for asters. This horticultural 'imbecility', as it is roundly named, links her with her husband's craziness and points clearly towards the inevitable failure of her marriage plans for Christopher. The latter, whom we have already met briefly at the tennis-party, is presented as an amiable but limply ineffectual young man who tinkers with a camera and has to be constantly reminded of his duty to Miss Hope-Drummond. He will come briefly to life only when he declares his love for Francie, thereby almost taking the reader as well as himself by surprise. In his gawky, epicene flaccidity he contrasts with Hawkins' casual and vulgar virility. Pamela, his sister, appears as the very epitome of well-bred insignificance. She sings in the choir, does her social duty in the village, is good-natured and kindly but seems marked for spinsterdom and is made to play only a tiny part in the book's complicated amours. Her shy swain, Captain Cursiter, never tells his love. As a group, the Dysarts are presented to us as being, at best, amiably ineffectual and, at worst, downright demented. They are a genteel group of aristocratic hybrids who represent sterility and decay at the top of the social hierarchy and contrast powerfully in this respect with the gross and thrusting social vigour of Roddy Lambert and Charlotte Mullen. Since Edith avowedly based the character of Lady Dysart on her own mother, it is perhaps not altogether surprising that Mrs Somerville had certain reservations about the novel on its first appearance. She may have been a more perceptive critic than was realised at the time, penetrating instinctively towards an understanding of the formidable criticism of their own class upon which Edith and Martin had embarked. It is a curious and unmistakeable part of their joint achievement that, at their best, they not only recreated their own beloved tribe but also memorably indicted it. This was an historical insight which they were to continue to display in all their major works, including the novels which were jointly planned but finally completed by Edith alone after Martin's death, such as *Mount Music* (1919) and *The Big House of Inver* (1925). The Dysarts of Bruff are the fore-runners of the Talbot-Lowrys of Mount Music and the Prendevilles of Inver.

Like all really good novels, this one provides us with a host of memorable occasions which settle in our memories and ensure the book's survival in our regard. The picnic to Innishochery Island, with its near-fatal climax when the *Daphne* capsizes on the homeward journey; the wonderfully comical amateur theatricals in Chapter XX, so funny in themselves but so socially ruinous for poor, silly Francie; Charlotte Mullen's deadly visit to the 'turkey-hen', Mrs Lambert, in Chapter XXXII; Francie's embarrassing stay at Bruff and her long and dreary exile in Bray; Charlotte's lonely fury, in Chapter XXXIX, when she receives Lambert's letter about his engagement to Francie; Francie's bleak encounter with Hawkins and the Dysarts on Kingstown pier; the violent climax of Francie's death, coming just as she is struggling to free herself of Hawkins—these are but a few of the more memorable passages in a book which is equally notable for its authors' conscientious attention to the depiction of a host of convincing minor characters, from the truculent Norry to the timid Cursiter, from the amiable Pamela to the languidly disdainful Evelyn Hope-Drummond. The brilliant surface of the novel holds our constant attention, yet, again and again, we are made aware of Charlotte Mullen's malign and covert machinations which, in the long run, cost her what she most passionately desires. She is the great, central achievement of the novel. Ugly, bonhomous, managerial, grasping, intelligent, ruthlessly selfish, she lurches through the work, a figure of cumulative evil whose lustful desire for Roddy Lambert makes her even more dangerous because more vulnerable. Her peculiar menace is conveyed to us in animal imagery which further dehumanises her. At the opening of Chapter XXXIX, she is likened to some strange submarine beast:

> The movements of Charlotte's character, for it cannot be said to possess the power of development, were akin to those of some amphibious thing, whose strong, darting course under the water is only marked by a bubble or two, and it required almost an animal instinct to note them. Every bubble betrayed the creature below, but people never thought of looking out for these indications in Charlotte, or suspected that she had anything to conceal.

Later, when she is engaged in exposing Roddy Lambert's financial misdoings to Christopher Dysart, in Chapter XLVII, her voice reaches Cursiter in his launch on the lake and seems to him 'like the gruff barking of a dog'. The most effective aspect of the writers' depiction of Charlotte is the way in which we are prepared throughout the novel for her ultimate undoing of herself. The climax leaves her exposed to Lambert as the secret enemy who has contrived his downfall, at the precise moment when Lambert's new freedom, consequent on Francie's death, has made him available as a husband yet again. As these two finally confront each other in the potato-loft at Gurthnamuckla, with Francie lying dead on the road outside, the writers achieve a moment of multiple and terrible resonances which continue to echo unforgettably in the reader's mind. They had, as we have seen, experienced much difficulty about the ending of the novel and had hesitated to kill off the 'wild bird that had trusted itself' to them. Yet, like so much else in the book, the manner of her death is consistent with her portrayal throughout. It has, in a real sense, been prepared for by many of the earlier scenes in which Francie is depicted as a perilously risky rider, whether of horses or of bicycles. She makes a compellingly attractive figure on a horse, in her pencil-slim riding-habit, but her appearance is not matched by any skill. Charlotte describes her as 'no great shakes of a rider'. Death touches her when the *Daphne* founders, and Christopher will be haunted later by 'the white face rising and dipping in the trough of the grey lake waves'. She comes a cropper rather more amusingly when she falls off Mr Corkran's tricycle, to that gentleman's embarrassment, in Chapter XI. The many tumbles she takes prepare us for the final, fatal fall.

The Real Charlotte made the two cousins known to the literary world of their day. When Violet Martin visited Edinburgh early in the year after its publication, she found herself treated with considerable respect by such literary notables as Andrew Lang. The new novel was thought to resemble Balzac's *La Cousine Bette* which, as it happened, neither Edith nor Martin had yet read. They ought now to have moved on to the writing of further major works of fiction and clearly wanted to do so. Edith makes clear, in *Irish Memories,* that they thought about writing another 'serious novel' but a variety of circumstances combined to prevent their doing so. The enormous success of the first volume of the 'R.M.' stories in 1899 diverted them from the longer form of the novel and their literary agent, J. B. Pinker, was to press them constantly to produce yet more stories of the 'R.M.' type. They made more money by such work and short stories were composed more speedily than long, serious novels, though it is clear that they often found Pinker's demands tiresome and tended to fob him off by putting together extempore collections of short stories already published in various magazines. Then, late in 1898, disaster struck when Martin was dreadfully injured in a fall from her horse, 'Dervish', while out hunting. She took a long time to make even a partial recovery and the fall may have hastened her death in 1915. Edith was to do some excellent work on her own but, if Martin had lived, the two of them, working together with the extraordinary mutual sympathy which was the essence of their collaboration, might have illuminated the new Ireland with that combination of historical instinct and moral profundity that they had brought to bear on the old Ireland in the pages of *The Real Charlotte.*

Selected Bibliography

RELATED WORKS
An Irish Cousin, London, 1889.
Mount Music, London, 1919.
The Big House of Inver, London, 1925 (pbk rpt Quartet Books, 1978).
The Real Charlotte is currently available in pbk form from Quartet Books
Ltd, London.

BIOGRAPHY
Geraldine Cummins, *Dr E. Œ. Somerville: A Biography, 1952.*
Maurice Collis, *Somerville and Ross: A Biography,* London, 1968.

CRITICAL STUDIES
Violet Powell, *The Irish Cousins,* London, 1970.
John Cronin, *Somerville and Ross,* Lewisburg, 1972.

CRITICAL ARTICLES
Ann Power, "The Big House of Somerville and Ross", *The Dubliner* (Spring
1964), 43-53.
Thomas Flanagan, "The Big House of Ross-Drishane", *The Kenyon Review*
(Jan. 1966), 54-78.
Sean McMahon, "John Bull's Other Island: A Consideration of *The Real
Charlotte* by Somerville and Ross", *Eire-Ireland* (Winter 1968), 119-135.

Index